LIBRARIES
AS
COMMUNICATION
SYSTEMS

J. M. Orr

*Contributions in Librarianship
and Information Science, Number 17*

Greenwood Press
Westport, Connecticut • London, England

Library of Congress Cataloging in Publication Data

Orr, James McConnell.
    Libraries as communications systems.

    (Contributions in librarianship and information
science ; no. 17)
    Includes bibliographical references and index.
    1. Libraries. 2. Library science-Philosophy.
3. System theory. I. Title. II. Series.
Z665.O76   020'.1   76-8739
ISBN 0-8371-8936-5

The quote on pages 180-81 is from Johnny Speight, *It Stands to Reason:
A Kind of Autobiography,* published by Michael Joseph Ltd., 1973, and
is reprinted with permission.

Library of Congress Catalog Card Number: 76-8739
ISBN: 0-8371-8936-5

First published in 1977

Greenwood Press, Inc.
51 Riverside Avenue, Westport, Connecticut 06880

Printed in the United States of America

Societies have always been shaped more by the nature of the media by which men communicate than by the content of the communication.
Marshall McLuhan

Of making many books there is no end and much study is a weariness of the flesh.
Ecclesiastes

Contents

Preface

This work is an outgrowth of a thesis submitted at the University of Strathclyde, Glasgow, Scotland. The reason for the choice of topic will be of interest to readers, perhaps particularly to any who may be embarking on thesis work and hope to find a subject for study which will take them to the frontiers of knowledge and perhaps reward them with the excitement of startling new discoveries. I was certainly hopeful of finding such a topic since, throughout a number of years of rather intensive academic lecture programs, I had been called upon to cover, in general if not specific terms, almost every conceivable topic of librarianship. Some possibilities had to be rejected on the practical basis that they required much more field work than I could feasibly manage, others because I feared that I lacked the necessary motivation to sustain the dicipline.

By a stroke of good luck I was, while in the course of making the decision, introduced to the subject of general systems theory, a discipline attempting to find common principles among all disciplines—the natural sciences, technology, the social sciences, and the humanities. On investigation, I found that this could be a most helpful tool to use in the construction of a general philosophy of libraries and librarianship. On reflection, I decided that this would be good for me, offering the opportunity of organizing many random ventures from previous work.

The fact that the work has now been redrafted for publication is gratifying; it is especially pleasing that it is to be included in the Contributions in Librarianship and Information Science series because it is offered exactly as that—a contribution— and no more. There are no sensational disclosures to be found in this book. Rather it is a new look at, and construction of, many well-discussed topics. Because of this general treatment, the specialist may be disappointed with the coverage of his pet topic, but he may find a new perspective on it, whether that perspective agrees with mine or not. To those who share my perspective of librarianship, I do not offer complacency because, in the course of continuing seminar debates and discussions with students and colleagues, I find the view subtly altered from time to time.

My hope, therefore, is that this work will be accepted for what it was intended to be—a contribution—and I will be more than glad to receive comments from colleagues on either general or specific matters. I also hope that some readers may find areas which will stimulate them to further research; there is much to be done.

In choosing examples of present-day library practice, it was natural for me to concentrate on the United Kingdom, although significant foreign (particularly American) practice is often quoted. In redrafting, I was strongly tempted to replace the examples from the United Kingdom with American ones, but on reflection I felt that this would be quite wrong, not only because I would obviously have been less sure of their aptness but also because I am sure that American colleagues will be happy to accept them and may find interest in replacing them with comparative examples from their own knowledge. If I have chosen badly and reached wrong conclusions, I will be glad to hear of it.

Frequent reference is made to the national libraries of the United Kingdom, and American readers should be cautioned about terminology. In 1973 the British Library was constituted, not as a new library but as an administrative amalgamation of the existing British Museum Library, the National Central Library, the National Lending Library of Science and Technology, and the British National Bibliography. The new library has organized itself into divisions, and the British Museum Library has become the British Library, Reference Division, and the National Central Library and the National Lending Library of Science and Technology have joined forces to become the British Library, Lending Division. When quoting examples which were obtained under the old order, I have retained the old terminology, but the new names are used to refer to the current situation.

The debt that I owe to libraries and books as sources of information will be obvious, the debt to colleagues, students and staff alike, less so. To the many hundreds of them who have continually stimulated much of the work which is now presented, this book is dedicated with many thanks.

Part One

THE FUNDAMENTALS

1
Systems Theory

Systems theory is scientific in nature in that it uses an analytical approach to determine the constituent parts of the whole, thus contributing to a better understanding of a system. It is doubtful if it is scientific in that it formulates laws which will govern all situations. The reasons for this doubt will become apparent when some of the concepts of the theory are applied to libraries as systems. From this point of view, it is more of a quasi-science. Nevertheless, it allows one to examine further the concept of a library and to formulate a base philosophy from which an organization may be built.

Since K. E. Boulding in 1956 attempted to outline facets of a general theory which would apply to all systems, workers in various disciplines, but particularly management theorists, have been applying the concept of a general theory to specific situations.[1]

This intellectual process is a reaction against the ever-increasing specialization of knowledge. To quote Boulding:

> The spread of specialised deafness means that someone who ought to know something that someone else knows isn't able to find it out for lack of generalised ears.

> It is one of the major objectives of General Systems Theory to develop these generalised ears, and by developing a frame-work of general theory to enable one specialist to catch relevant communications from others.[2]

The general nature of the theory is simplicity itself. All disciplines or structures consist of populations composed of individuals or parts which connect together to form the whole, or the system. The connection between the parts—the "binding" which holds them together—can always be interpreted as information which is communicated from part to part. The process of analyzing the whole into its constituent parts and determining what the information is, and how it is communicated leads to a much greater understanding of the functions and objectives of the system and makes it easier to pinpoint any malfunction which may arise.

As a brief and tentative introduction to how this process works, the remainder of this first chapter will comment on some of the laws of general systems theory and relate them in particular to libraries as systems. This will allow preliminary speculation about the basic purpose of libraries and possible areas of malfunction.

Preparatory to this examination, it is assumed that the parts of a library system may be grouped into three main areas: people (staff and readers); recorded communications within the library; and buildings, furniture, and equipment (or, in reverse order, hardware, software, and humanware).

LAW 1

Individuals prefer states and, if disturbed, tend to try to regain equilibrium or homeostasis.

This is a law which is more applicable to the physical sciences than the social sciences. It may well be that the inherent goal of a society of humans is stability, but the whole history of revolution and war seems to suggest that the effort of attempting to obtain it paradoxically creates a constant state of flux. Since libraries must reflect society, they also are in a state of flux, or at least the knowledge collected by them is. Basically, the law holds good in that probably everyone would like a utopian situation in which knowledge is absolute, certain, and unchanging, but man is a goal-seeking animal and in his search he is constantly making new discoveries which add to or change his present knowledge. Libraries must reflect these changes insofar as they are recorded in the media which libraries collect. The history of the political and religious censorship of the written word proves this point. In almost every instance, the reason for the attempted ban was to protect the status quo of knowledge as determined by some establishment. At least in the democratic countries, the right to change knowledge or attitudes to knowledge has been won. Libraries, in reflecting this knowledge, also change and would seem to be an exception to this law.

LAW 2

Individuals interact with environment and exhibit:
a. behavior
b. action
c. change

The study of this law in relation to human psychology has become a discipline in its own right—the behavioral sciences—and it needs no stretch of the imagination to see that people do react to particular situations in which they find themselves. As users of libraries they react much more favorably to an open-access stock than to a closed-access stock; that is, they make much more use of open-access stock. Even the increased theft of stock sustains this example. The whole process of the planning and design of a library building is dependent on this law. The problem is to create an environment in which the interaction between readers and stock will be most easily and effectively accomplished. The stock too has to "behave" in that its presentation to the reader shall be fully advantageous. The methods used to display stock are of strong interest to the practicing librarian. Problems of how to classify stock into an order helpful to readers has been one of the major areas of study, and problems of physical arrangement, particularly of nonbook media, are of considerable importance.

The purpose of creating this behavior is to lead the "action" of a reader's contact with information and knowledge which, in turn, can lead to "change." Readers presumably change in that they acquire more understanding, even if it be at a gratification level, and some will, because of this, create further knowledge in the form of a medium which can be stored in libraries, and this creates change in the stock of the library. This process describes admirably a feedback, or cyclic, system which is often found in systems analysis. It could be that this is the most important purpose of a library.

LAW 3

The behavior of an individual is explained by the structure of individuals of which it is composed.

If Law 2 is supported by the example of the behavioral sciences, then Law 3 is supported by hereditary examples. Animals with wings are meant to fly, with legs to walk, or with fins to swim. In terms of libraries, one can say that if a particular library has "inherited" media on only one particular subject, then it can only "behave" within the limits of the media it stores, the readers it attracts, and the facilities it provides. A reference library can cause only the "action" of reader meeting medium within its walls since, by definition, it will not lend its stock for home reading. As part of its system, study tables and chairs must be introduced as "individuals."

LAW 4

Systems are either deterministic or probabilistic.

The theory here is that if one views systems in terms of what is put into them, relating this to what comes out, it is possible to say in some instances what the output will be, whereas in others it will be almost impossible. A computer is a good example of a deterministic system. It is a machine which will perform only in accordance with the codes or programs which are fed into it. Therefore, provided that we program correctly and there is no malfunction, we can determine what the output will be. A library, on the other hand, is quite the opposite. One can determine only in a very loose fashion that the higher the quality and, up to a point, the greater the quantity of "individuals" which we put into a library, the greater the use will be. Even then, this would only be a quantitative determination: it does not go very far in determining the amount of change effected, which, as shown by Law 2, is one way of looking at the basic purpose of a library.

The conception of a probabilistic system has led to the management theory of the "black box".[3] The principle involved is that a manager of a system which is so complex that the interaction of its individuals cannot be comprehended fully or controlled can manage only by controlling input and carefully quantifying output. A librarian as a manager is at an even greater disadvantage in that he can only make inspired guesses as to the quality of his output.

The "black box" is neatly summed up by the following poem by Boulding:

A system is a big black box
Of which we can't unlock the locks
And all we can find out about
Is what goes in and what comes out.

Perceiving input-output pairs,
Related by parameters,
Permits us sometimes, to relate
An input, output, and a state.

If this relation's good and stable
Then to predict we may be able,
But if this fails us—heaven forbid!
We'll be compelled to force the lid![4]

LAW 5

Growth is an important pattern of behavior.

This is a rather obvious statement, of particular validity in relation to living systems. All would seem to change by growth, both in the short term by the growth of the individual and in the long term by evolutionary growth. It is possible that man injects a similar pattern of behavior into his man-made systems. It would certainly be true of his libraries. As his knowledge has expanded, his libraries have reflected the growth. The exponential nature of this growth is shown by the following estimate.[5]

	Birth of Christ		
First doubling of knowledge	to 1750	=	1,750 years
Second doubling of knowledge	1750-1900	=	250 years
Third doubling of knowledge	1900-1950	=	50 years
Fourth doubling of knowledge	1950-1960	=	10 years
Fifth doubling of knowledge	1960-1966	=	6 years

The growth factor of a system is an important management conception since it creates many administrative problems which must be overcome if the increase in size is not to stifle the original purpose of the system.
It is a factor which plays a large part in the development of libraries.

LAW 6

The dynamic relationships between individuals are either:

a. parasitic
b. competitive
c. complementary

It is easy to find examples to fit this law. All games are competitive
systems, one team attempting to score more goals than the other in order
to win. It may well be argued that games devised by human beings are
substitutes for animal territorial battles, and it is interesting to note how
games have been introduced into management education in order to simu-
late situations in commerce, which is a highly competitive system. From a
different discipline, a complementary system is the cooling system of an
internal combustion engine: it is additional to the main system, an essential
adjunct to it if it is going to function properly.

The most obvious examples of parasitic systems are bacteriological
diseases of man. Since these are harmful and often lethal, they have been
subjected to analysis to determine when they are the cause of a malfunction
of a human system so that a cure may be found.

Parasitic relationships are not necessarily harmful, the mammalian method
of birth being a good example of a nonharmful type.

It is possible to argue that a library system as part of the system of the
social organization of man has something of all three relationships. Such
an argument shows some of the shortcomings of an analytical approach
which creates linear categories which appear to be mutually exclusive yet
prove not to be so in practice. Such analyses are often oversimplifications
of a complex situation, yet paradoxically they can help to show some of
the system's complexities and at the same time focus attention on its important aspects.

At first glance, it might appear that a library system is not parasitic but
that certain aspects of it are. It could cynically be pointed out that a num-

ber of librarians have had nervous breakdowns because of psychological stress in overconscientiously attempting to cope with the organization of a system with an exponential growth rate. It could equally be pointed out that the creation of books can also cause problems because books are psychologically parasitic on their authors. More important is the contention made by many people that "bad" (or "obscene") books can morally pollute a society. The tremendous range of laws passed by various nations in an attempt to cure the parasite of moral pollution testifies to the strength of this view. As previously noted, parasitic subsystems are not necessarily harmful to the host system, a fetus being an obvious example. The analogy with libraries is that they are the children of society living on the thought content fed to them by the members of society. Individual libraries also parasitically use the stock of other libraries via interloan schemes when their own stock is lacking.

Another aspect of this law is that much of the knowledge contained in the majority of works in a library has been cannibalized from other works. From a purely scientific point of view, this means that much of the information in a library store is redundant in that it is repeated in many works; on the other hand, it could be held that while the message is the same, it is necessary to change its form and style to suit different tastes and to make different impacts. As an example of this, one might cite the area of literary criticism. *Hamlet* has possibly been subjected to more detailed analysis than any other single work, yet while fundamental approaches change little, critics still believe they may add to the understanding of the work by further detailed criticism. As society has become more affluent, it has been able to release more and more of its members for the purpose of writing. The librarian may be of two minds about this problem in that he welcomes more and more information because on the whole it helps his retrieval problem, but he shudders at the administrative problems which the expanded growth holds for him.

It is also possible to see a competitive relationship in libraries. In one sense, libraries, by disseminating knowledge, compete or battle with the existence of prejudice and bigotry. Philosophers at all levels have often seen the situation of mankind in terms of his ever-increasing knowledge, which overcomes the ignorance of prejudice and bigotry. Similar arguments were often used by the promoters of libraries who saw in them a major force in the struggle of society against these abstract enemies. Sadly, there is little evidence that they have been outstandingly effective.

In another sense, libraries compete with other systems of mass communication. In this sense the competitive nature of a library system is becoming increasingly more important in the twentieth-century scientific and technological era, which has provided other mass media which communicate to the public at large. It might be thought that the library should be a complementary system to these and to a great extent it is, but it is equally competitive in that most of the other media are strongly motivated by commercial interests. It may be very important to society that this commercialization be counterbalanced by a system which is not so motivated.

However, it is clear that the more important concept of a library is that of a complementary system. Perhaps man's most important subsystem is his communicating system, which has developed to such a degree that he has accomplished the graphic creation of records which are capable of being stored. Having created the records, he naturally then created the store he uses to protect and keep them. Libraries thus become complementary communication systems to his own communicatory system.

LAW 7

An understanding of the communications between individuals is essential for a full comprehension of the system.

This would seem to be complementary to Law 4. In a deterministic system, such as a computer, the nature of the communication is sufficiently understood to allow an estimate of the output to be made, at least in terms of the amount of characters, if not their precise meaning. Their meaning still has to be interpreted. In a library system, the full nature of the communication between book and reader is less well understood and can only be probabilistic. The example of censorship of books is illustrative. Censors argue that "bad" books can harm and therefore they must be eliminated, and anticensors argue that there is no real evidence that a book has harmed, the "bad" being inherent in the reader rather than the book. This argument to some extent can be rationalized in terms of a feedback or cyclic system. The badness must be inherent in man since he is the creator of his recorded communications. If some men introduce this badness into their books, then this feeds back to others who read it. The way in which this communication affects them is less clearly understood. Some will not be affected because, out of naivete, they do not perceive the badness. Others will fully recognize it for what it is, perhaps even experiencing a short-term vicarious gratification, but reject the concept as a way of life, while others may wish to relive the gratification in realistic terms. It would appear that, in our present state of knowledge, it is impossible to determine to what degree individual persons or groups of persons are so affected.

It is interesting to compare the laws of general systems theory with the five laws of library science as propounded by S. R. Ranganathan. These are:

1. Books are for use.
2. Every book its reader.
3. Every reader its book.
4. Save the time of the reader.
5. A library is a growing organism.[6]

The first four of Ranganathan's laws are simple statements which emphasize that the purpose of any library is to bring a reader into contact with the books and communications he needs either consciously or unconsciously. They are summarized in the more general terms of systems theory by Law 2, "Individuals interact with environment . . . ." The fundamental purpose of a library is to promote the interaction of book and reader. Ranganathan's fifth law is clearly the same as Law 5, "Growth is an important pattern of behavior."

POSTULATE

Summing up the above attempt to relate some of the concepts of general systems theory to libraries, it is possible to postulate the following:

Above all, a library is a knowledge-communicatory system which reflects man's own knowledge system. It is, therefore, a complementary feedback system which exists to encourage the action of book meeting reader, with possible changes being effected. Because of the nature of its feedback, it is exponential in growth. Because it is a man-made system, it operates only as man manages it, but it is probabilistic in output. In some of its aspects it is competitive with other media.

NOTES

1. Boulding, K. E., "General Systems Theory: The Skeleton of a Science,"
   Management Science 2 (1956), pp. 197-208; Hanika, F. de P., *New Thinking
   in Management: A Guide for Managers* (Hutchison, 1965), pp. 8-15.
2. Boulding, K. E., "General Systems Theory," pp. 197-208.
3. Beer, S., *Cybernetics and Management* (EUP, 1959).
4. Mesarovic, M. D., ed., *Views on General Systems Theory* (Wiley,1964), p. 39.
5. Murgio, M. P., *Communications Graphics* (Van Nostrand, 1969), p. 199.
6. Ranganathan, S. R., *Five Laws of Library Science,* 2nd ed. (Blunt, 1957).

2
Comparative Analysis of Three Communication Systems

The communication of information among individuals within a system is an essential part of any system. The output of systems is similarly important to other systems, though the information communicated will be of different kinds according to the type of system. For instance, any building communicates information as to its use, possibly by its exterior architecture and certainly by the configuration of the rooms within it. Each room in turn declares its purpose by the layout of furniture and equipment within it, and each of these units tends to show its function. Such information may be considered latent. The output of a machine is power and this can be quantified in many ways according to the type of power and the reason for the quantification.

Man can be analyzed in terms of a machine and his output calculated, but his interest to us here lies in his capacity as an organism capable of an output of information in the more accepted meanings of the word, that is, knowledge and data. This is our interest, since his libraries complement him as a communication system.

It would, therefore, seem relevant to attempt an analysis of man from this point of view, relating this to his library system. It is proposed to add to this a comparison between a computer and man and his libraries, since there is a strong prima facie case for maintaining that the computer is, or certainly could be, his greatest technological communicatory tool, and the likelihood is that much of the future development of libraries may depend on its application to the library system.

It is not proposed to analyze in detail any of these systems, since this would lead to a complete study of behavioral psychology, library science, and computer science, all of which are extremely complex systems. It

will be sufficient to make a broad comparative analysis which will underline the advantages and disadvantages of each, taking refuge in the following statement: "The system theorist of the future, I suggest, must be an
expert in how to simplify."[1] The following, therefore, is a simple analysis of man (or any other animal) as a communicatory system.

At the stimulus end of the system, he:
   1. perceives
   2. receives
   3. recognizes
   4. retains
At the response end, he:
   5. retrieves
   6. relays
   7. re-creates

In perceiving his environment, man uses all of his senses of sight, hear-
ing, smell, taste, and touch. The information which is sensed is transmitted
to the brain where it is received and recognized. The distinction between
reception and recognition is rather subtle and is of passing interest in this
context. Recognition obviously must be a second or later reception of a
message since the first can only be received—if it is understood, it is only
in an instinctive way. For example, the first reception of the danger of
fire is by touch, and the nervous system warns the brain of this danger to
the physical body. Future receptions, together with recognition or understanding of this phenomenon, may be sensed by sight. There is an opposite
example of the relationship between reception and recognition. Constant
reception of a stimulus may almost completely dull the senses to recognition of it to the extent that a consciousness or recognition that the stimulus was being received is apparent only when the stimulus is removed. The
use of background music and the sudden cessation of the noise of raindrops
on a window are examples.

Although modern psychology has explained, to some extent, the complex relationships hinted at above, it is clearly seen that a great deal still
has to be discovered. If this is true for this part of the system, it is more
so for the retentive and retrieval parts of the system. This, of course, is
the psychology of memory, perhaps the least understood part of the
system and one which has engaged the minds of education psychologists
because it plays such a large part in the learning process.

What is fairly clear is that modern education is tending to move away

from an attitude which sees the mind purely as a storage and retrieval device and is beginning to concentrate more on how the mind relays and
reacts to stimuli. The simple fact is that the human brain is a rather poor
storage device in comparison with other tools which man has devised, at
least in the quantitative aspect. It is possibly better to leave the storage of
data to those other tools, leaving the human mind freer to re-create from
the information received.

If the systems of library and computer are compared with the human system, this point should become clearer. Table 1 tentatively shows the
relationship.

Analogies are obviously stretched in some comparisons. To suggest
that a library (i. e., its staff) selects its materials in the same way that
man senses a stimulus is perhaps somewhat farfetched. Yet even this
analogy is pertinent to theory. Man's senses are stimulated by his total
environment, and if he has to perform to his utmost capacity, there should
be no malfunction in his senses to the extent that information is not received. It can be argued analogously that if a library is a complementary
system to man, then it in turn cannot afford to ignore any stimulus. In
other words, since its purpose is to collect and put to use man's recorded
communications, it must not malfunction by eschewing any of them.

What is most striking in the comparison of the three systems is the
strong analogy in the area of memory. All three are obviously stores of
knowledge and if anything has to happen to the data, it must be retrieved
from the store. The analogy almost ends there. Each of the three memory
systems is quite different. On any quantitative basis, man's system is
the poorest.

It has been calculated that man can think of only about 100 bits (binary digits) of information at one time and that his span of absolute
errorless judgment extends to some 10 bits.[2] His quick-access memory
is thus poor and his channel capacity is low. Taking 200 pages as the
average length of books, there are some 10^6 characters used in each.[3]
Assuming that the largest library has the equivalent of some 10 million
books, it therefore stores 10^{13} characters or $2 \cdot 10^{14}$ bits at 12 bits per
character. While it has not yet been possible to quantify man's permanent memory it must be very considerably lower than this figure: a pro-
lific author may produce only 100 books or $2 \cdot 10^9$ bits. Thus, the value
of a library as a corporate memory of mankind is great. Currently, a computer may have a capacity of some 10^6 bits in its direct-access memory,

TABLE 1

	Function	Man	Library	Computer
Stimulus/Input	Perception		Selects	
	Reception	Senses	Acquires	Accepts man-made signals and codes
	Recognition	Understands		
	Retention	Memorizes	Stores	Stores
	Retrieval	Remembers	Finds items by indexing methods	Recalls signals as programmed to do so
	Relay	Communicates	Allows access	Delivers print-outs
Response/Output	Re-creation	Invents		

but, with the addition of backing stores, this can be increased to such an extent that it could theoretically be capable of storing the quantitative store of a large library and perhaps the totality of knowledge. In retrieving from the memory store, man must also be the poorest system because he stores less information. He is also much slower than a computer when a bulk of data is required as opposed to a single fact. If his memory does not store a fact, he may find it very quickly in his library system since his experience with the sources in the library endow him with a certain flair for retrieval, and such retrieval could be much quicker than programming a computer.

Another striking and important aspect of the comparison is the action of re-creation. This could be viewed philosophically as the really important end product of a communication system. Despite the obvious necessity in all systems to relay to others what has been processed through the system, a deeper and more important function is achieved if the data retrieved are processed within the system and rearranged in such a way that new knowledge or data is re-created. Only man is capable of doing this. It could be argued that a library, in arranging or classifying its items in a certain way, can throw new light on certain topics, but it is only as this is conveyed to the mind of man that it is effective. It can also be pointed out that a computer can output data with tremendous speed in almost limitless permutations, but if this has to begin to make any sense, then it must be programmed so that there is some restriction on complete randomness. Even then the output is mechanical and value judgments are the prerogative of the mind of man. From this point of view, man is the only true cyclic, or feedback, system of the three. It is he who feeds his own mind, it is he who replenishes his libraries with new ideas and concepts, and only he can program the computer.

Arthur Koestler propounded a theory that in all instances the inventiveness of man proceeds from an association of ideas taken often from supposedly different disciplines.[4] The ideas are reconnected, or re-created, to form a new concept. One of the examples he chose to illustrate this was the invention of the printing press. It is just theoretically possible that the ideas which led to this invention could have been brought together in a library or by a computer, but, beyond a shadow of a doubt, neither could have seen the value of the information. Neither, of course, could many a human mind, but at least one did: the ideas were made practical and civilization was significantly changed.

Man, therefore, is the master system, and it is his ability to create which has led him to complement his own communication system with other communicatory tools which he manufactures, to some extent, in the image of his own system and which he manipulates to his own ends. His power to develop in this fashion is a fascinating story and mystery, worthy of separate treatment in the next chapter.

NOTES

1. Ashby, W. R., "Introductory Remarks at a Panel Discussion," in Mesarovic, M. D., *Views on General Systems Theory* (Wiley, 1964), pp. 165-169.
2. Miller, G. A., *Psychology of Communications* (Penguin, 1970), p. 54.
3. Licklider, J. C. R., *Libraries of the Future* (MIT Press, 1965), p. 15.
4. Koestler, A., *The Act of Creation* (Hutchinson, 1964), pp. 121-123.

3

Development of Man's Communication Systems

Libraries are complementary systems to man, and, before embarking on their development, which runs concurrently with man's own development as a graphic communicator, it is interesting to speculate on his own development as the most highly sophisticated communicatory animal species. Much of the story must be speculation since, up until the time man began to record graphically, we have only palaeontological and archaeological evidence, coupled with inspired guesses. The guesswork must be based on an acceptance of the Darwinian theory of evolution: the natural selection of species by environment whereby species change anatomically and psysiologically to meet their changing surroundings. The evidence now available to support this theory is now so great that there is an almost general acceptance. Most of the proof of the development of man by the evolutionary process comes from the fossilized remains of skeletons and, from later times, the remains of his tools. Archaeologists and anthropologists have now fitted together a very remarkable history which is acceptable in broad terms, although they would be the first to admit that there are detailed differences of opinion and some speculation must still take place in assigning dates.

Even if evolutionary theory is not accepted, it is clear that present-day *Homo sapiens* is king. He is so far in advance of any other species in his achievement of making an environment suit him that some explanation is demanded.

By natural selection or some other means, man is gifted. The gift is a superior brain which allows him much greater scope than any other species in the creation of ideas. The ideas may remain in the abstract or they may be created in reality. All of his physical creations can be conceived of as being tools which he uses to extend the limited capacities of his own mind and body. The branch of a tree is an extension of the arm, the computer an extension of the brain. It can be argued that other species use tools, and this is true at the elementary level of using branches, stones, or other natural implements. But no other species has the forethought to shape the implements into artifacts more specifically suited to particular tasks or to keep the tool for future use.

It is this gift of forethought which, more than anything else, distinguishes man; it is this which spurs him to greater advances and more and more complex and sophisticated tools.

It is this, too, which creates the human predicament of a concept of morality, of good and evil. Forethought allows man a concept of death which is probably unique among species and leads to complex burial rituals and, more ominously, to murder. There is simply no parallel among the other species for the mass slaughter that modern warfare has perpetuated; they do not have the tools, and the examples of individual killing of members of the same species are few and far between.

The intricacies of philosophies of good and evil must be left to others, but it is worth noting their possible origins since the conflict between those two forces manifests itself in almost every facet of society. It is probably true that every tool ever devised could be used for either a virtuous or a deleterious objective. The choice is man's.

To a librarian, among the more direct consequences of man's supremacy are his tool-making activities, which produce not only the artifacts which he creates to make graphic communication possible but also the conceptual tools of language, alphabet, and other communication devices which have brought him to his preeminent position. Without the tools of communication, the other artifacts would have remained in a relatively simple form, and, but for the original artifacts of stone tools, the concept of communicatory tools would not have been possible.

In searching for a philosophy of librarianship, it is of rather obvious importance to have a clear understanding of the fundamental roots of the system. These lie in the evolution of communication tools and it is useful to trace the major steps.

We are faced with an immediate difficulty in so doing because it is impossible to state categorically whether oral communication (at least in an elementary articulated fashion) predated or postdated graphic communication. The cave paintings of some 20,000 years ago furnish the earliest evi-

dence, but, since tools were used long before this time, it seems a reasonable supposition that at some early stage they were used to communicate
messages graphically. As a general rule, man takes the easy way to do
things, and it appears certain that he first drew on the more pliable and
workable ground, but, of course, no records of this remain.

When and why he developed articulated speech is even more of a mystery. There is no evidence to sustain a biological theory of language.[1]
There are no extant primitive languages, all present-day languages being
relatively complex so that we cannot determine their origins.

So far, the greatest achievement in teaching language to animals has
been with the chimpanzee Washoe.[2] After some two years of training,
Washoe had a vocabulary of about thirty words in sign, not spoken,
language. He could also articulate some of these words into brief sentences,
a very considerable breakthrough despite the fact that it only highlights
the immense advance of man. All animals communicate, but they do so
in the main by visual, olfactory, and tactile signals of different kinds,
displaying emotions of fear, aggressiveness, and courtship.

Vocal signals are the prerogative of the more highly evolved species and,
in the main, can be interpreted as an accidental by-product of bodily gest-
ures giving information on emotion. These signals communicate to others
in an incidental but important manner. Vervet monkeys appear to have
at least six different alarm calls for different predators, and these stimulate different escape patterns. Man's achievement is that he makes a
conscious rather than an instinctual effort to communicate. It must
basically be this which led to articulation.

Lacking a sound biological theory, one is forced to attempt to explain the origins of language by sociological suppositions. If the articulation derives from a conscious effort to communicate, this effort must
be made to communicate with other individuals of his species with whom
he is cooperating for some mutual benefit. The main motivation for the
need for language lies in group activities, and it would seem that the
best explanation lies in the need to hunt and work. Man may well have
begun to imitate the natural sounds of his prey, either as a lure or to
communicate to a fellow hunter. The existence of words like "quack,"
"cuckoo," and "peewit" are taken as evidence of this. Probably more acceptable is the work theory. The need to hunt together in order to survive
naturally led to working together, and very often there was need for communicatory commands. At first, this would have been done by gesture,

but, since man was more often than not using his hands to work, he may well have gestured with his mouth and created special sounds. These would have proven useful when his fellows could not see him at night or when his back was turned.[3]

Whatever the basic motivation for conscious communication, it is clear that man's brain was at a sufficiently advanced stage to give him some realization of the importance of his new tool so that it became inevitable that he should make improvements in this just as he also improved his material tools. Since we have no fossil evidence of language, we can have no natural history of it, but to relate it to the natural history of tools seems apposite. Both are examples of man using his brain rather than his genes in his evolutionary progress.

By the beginning of the fourth millennium B.C., man was already in a preeminent position. He was capable of advanced articulated language communications and of making relatively advanced tools from stone and metal, so that his technology was now capable of altering his environment to suit his own ends. He was then poised for further progress, and this came in his communications, an advance which cannot be explained by biological theory, or absolute necessity for physical survival. It seems that man was fully committed to an intellectual evolution, and on this plane it can be claimed that his greatest achievement was the development of writing.

The earliest extant graphic records, the cave paintings, cannot be claimed to be systematic writing. They are mainly depictions of man's environment, but often with exaggerated symbolism, suggesting sympathetic magic. Occasionally, they were put in such inaccessible places that one can only surmise that the artist alone was meant to see them. Here is the first visible sign of man's affluence—he was treating his environment with artistic sympathy.

There is no evidence of systematic scripts prior to about the middle of the fourth millennium B.C., and our earliest extant records come from southern Mesopotamia. The Sumerian culture had begun to make records on clay tablets which were undoubtedly used mainly for building purposes. When soft, the tablet was ideal for writing; when hard, ideal for preservation. More than one thousand of these were unearthed in an excavation at Uruk. In its early stages, the Sumerian script was purely pictographic, consisting of pictures representing and meaning only the actual object which was drawn. From this early, simple, and cumbersome method, the mainstream development of writing can be traced with relative ease. We now have records which contain much of the evidence that we need. There are still many problems of decipherment of some early scripts and there is still conjecture about possible relationships and links between different scripts, but the main principles of the development are clear.

On the one hand, there was the need for more complexity because more information and more concepts had to be communicated. On the other hand, there was a need for more simplicity in order to speed the task of writing and to ease the task of reading. The development of a more complex system was the first step. Pictograms were meant to depict material things; in order to convey abstract concepts, it was necessary to symbolize the pictures so that they had to be interpreted as ideas rather than things. A simple example is that a drawing of a sun as a pictogram means just that, while the same drawing as an ideogram could also stand for concepts such as heat, light, and day. More information could be transmitted in ideograms, but at the cost of much possible confusion and loss of speed. Sumerian pictographic script soon acquired ideographic tendencies, and the urge for speed saw a steady conventionalization of ideograms which, since the writing was on clay tablets, took the shape of "wedges" because it was easier to impress marks on the clay rather than scratch them on. This script is known as cuneiform and forms one of the two major modes of writing of early civilization, the other being Egyptian hieroglyphics. Hieroglyphics ("holy writing") dates from about the beginning of the third millennium B.C. and there is some doubt as to whether it has any connection with cuneiform. Cuneiform predates it, but hieroglyphic script is anything but wedge-shaped. It was originally used for religious inscriptions on monumental stone and seems to have been artificially created for this purpose by someone with a knowledge of the principles of writing.

The major factor in the complexity of a script is the number of symbols necessary, and the progressive development of writing was one in which the large number of symbols in an ideographic script (900 in early Sumerian) was finally reduced to an alphabetic script of some twenty-two letters. The vital importance of the small number of symbols was underlined much later in the fifteenth century A.D. with the invention of moveable-type printing.

The early Sumerian script was developed by the introduction of the concept of symbols for sounds rather than symbols for pictures, and this phoneticism introduced a syllabic form of writing which reduced the number of symbols. About 2500 B.C. cuneiform was adopted by the Semites who lived in the Tigris-Euphrates Valley (i. e., the Babylonians and Assyrians). The Babylonians standardized the number of symbols at about 600 to 700 (about six vowel sounds, 300 syllables, and 300 ideograms). About the same time, the script was used by Elamites who abandoned their own script and, in adopting Babylonian cuneiform, reduced it to some 113 characters, of which over eighty were syllabic. Much later, around the sixth century B.C. the Persians adopted cuneiform and reduced it to a phonetic syllabary of forty-one symbols. This was the last great era of cuneiform; it rapidly became extinct in the early Christian era, mainly because it was second best to the outcome of another parallel development—the alphabet.

Before dealing with the alphabet, we should look briefly at the other great script of early civilization, Egyptian hieroglyphics. Its historical development was governed by the need for speed and ease of writing. The original formal inscriptional hieroglyphics evolved into a more cursive hieratic script for the purpose of writing on papyrus with a brush or pen, and this in turn, by about the seventh century B.C., developed into an even more cursive script, demotic hieroglyphics. This was a mixture of ideograms and phonograms, with some elements of alphabetization in that there were symbols for some single consonants. An alphabet did not, however, develop from this script, and until its end (about the fifth century A.D.) it remained a cumbersome script of many symbols. It would seem that this script remained very closely tied to the priestly cult and perhaps there was a tendency to keep it in a mysterious form. The changes in the script were changes in the shapes of the symbols rather than in the number of symbols.

From about 1000 B.C., the history of the alphabet is fairly clear, but its prehistory is obscure. A few fragments of an early Canaanite script of c. 1800 B.C. have been found. This has not been completely deciphered but apparently it was of alphabetic character. Around 1500 B.C. a cuneiform-shaped script of thirty-two letters appeared at Ugarit. This Canaanite script was probably influenced by an earlier Semitic alphabet but was adapted by a people who were used to writing on clay. It shows signs of deliberate invention. If this is so, the inventor (or inventors) can lay claim to being one of the greatest unsung heroes of the history of civilization.

From the eleventh century B.C., two main alphabetic scripts made their appearance, early Hebrew and Phoenician. Both had some twenty-two symbols, and it is from the Phoenician branch that the Latin alphabet, which we use today with slight modification, developed. The Phoenicians were great traders and they exported their alphabet with their goods, their inscriptions having been found in Cyprus, Malta, Sicily, Greece, Marseilles, and Spain. The survival of the alphabet was ensured when it was adopted by the Greeks and radically modified by their introduction of vowels. A number of peoples used Greek script (e. g., the Etruscans). In the late seventh century B.C., the Romans adapted it to the needs of Latin, using twenty-one of the twenty-six letters. In the first century B.C., they added the Greek symbols Y and Z and so established their basic alphabet of twenty-three letters, to which was added, in medieval times, the letters J, U, and W to make our present-day alphabet, which was carried to all parts of the world by the spread of Christianity and the power of European politics and culture.

And so for some 3,000 years, mankind, or at least part of mankind, has had at its disposal an extraordinary and efficient tool of communication in the form of an alphabet of between twenty and thirty symbols, relatively easily learned and written. It is with the use of this tool that man forges his new civilizations and new technologies. Having created his written records, he has to make sure that they are used by others, and it is in this sphere that libraries are all-important.

To underline the importance of the introduction of the alphabet to European civilization, it is only necessary to compare Western with Eastern civilization briefly. The early East produced significant achievements, particularly the inventions of gunpowder, the mariner's compass, and paper, but its most important invention, writing, remained ideographic, which undoubtedly retarded its progress. The earliest extant record of Chinese writing is dated c. 1500 B.C., at which stage there seems to have been some 2,500-3,000 characters in use. Because of the lack of development of an alphabet, this number has had to increase with the expansion of knowledge, and in modern-day Chinese there is a total of some 25,000-30-000 ideograms, although only about 2,000-5,000 are in constant use. Chinese script has the longest historical span, but its evolution has occurred mainly within China without foreign influence. The Chinese invention of paper in 105 A.D. provided a relatively cheap commodity which could be produced in an elementary form of mass production and in a seemingly infinite supply, the basic raw material being vegetable matter such as cotton, linen, and wood.

The use of paper spread slowly from China to the West. By 850 A.D. it was used in Egypt and Damascus, replacing papyrus by 950, spreading along the North Coast of Africa to Morocco by 1100 and entering Spain by 1150 and Italy by 1283. At this time, it was competing with another finer and stronger material, parchment. Parchment, made of the specially prepared skins of animals, had been introduced in the second century B.C., legend having it that its invention was the result of Egypt's having cut off the supply of papyrus to the king of Pergamum. It proved to be a particularly fine material for penmanship, and in the era when manuscripts were aesthetically embellished with decorative miniatures and illumination, it was often preferred to paper.

The invention of moveable type changed that. In many ways the invention of moveable type can be viewed as the first breakthrough in communications. The changes we have noted so far were gradual in two ways: it took time for the change itself to be implemented, and it also took time for its effect to be felt. Comparatively speaking, moveable-type printing was an explosion. Within the space of a decade, the basic technology was complete and within fifty short years printing presses were established throughout Europe. Whereas a scribe or scribes may well have taken many months of painstaking physical writing to produce one copy of a book, a printer could now "write" the words, using single pieces of type for each character, in a few weeks and, from this setting, produce as many copies as he thought fit, at a rate of production which completely overwhelmed that of the scribe. This is the first example of real mass production in the communications field; it ensured that mankind could fully disseminate his knowledge to all who wished to make use of it at an ever-decreasing cost in real terms. The art of printing from blocks had been practiced in China perhaps for as long as a thousand years, and indeed moveable print had been born in the ninth century A.D.—stillborn really, since the practical difficulties of applying the principle to a script of thousands of symbols was too great. There is absolutely no evidence that the moveable-type principle spread from East to West, but it is highly likely that block printing did. This was a method eminently suitable for illustrative drawings but not for words. To carve the letters of a text of any length was an even more time-consuming task than writing them, and despite the fact that many copies could be produced, it could only be copies of one text. The advantage of moveable type is that, after one text has been completed, the pieces of type can be redistributed and at some future time recomposed to form the necessary combinations of letters for another text.

As mentioned previously, this invention is one of the prime examples of the re-creative ability of man's mind. Only one real technological advance was needed since all other requirements for it were available. Relief printing from wood blocks was well-known, paper and ink available, the principle of the wine press well-established, and the practice of working and casting metal well-understood. The necessity, or at least the strong desirability of making the invention, must have also been in the minds of many.

Looking at the situation from the vastly superior technological position of the twentieth century, it is easy to say that it only needed someone to put all these ideas together and to make the one advance of creating a moveable mold which could be altered to suit the different sizes of body necessary to cast the different widths of letters of the alphabet. Easy perhaps, but in terms of the effect it had on future civilization, it still has a strong claim to being one of the greatest inventions of all time.[4]

Because of the ultimate significance of the invention, many claims have been put forward as to who was responsible. The strongest claim is for Johann Gutenberg, who undoubtedly experimented with the idea for a number of years and almost certainly had a very great deal to do with the production of the first printed book, a magnificent two-volume Bible. From a rubrication date on one copy of this work we know that it was completed sometime before August 1456, a date which deserves pride of place in any history but often does not get it because historians are too busy examining power struggles. However, it is not without significance that many historians date modern history from around this time. The cultural revolution of the Renaissance had begun earlier in Italy and, while it is doubtful that it was a major factor in motivating the invention of moveable type, it is clear that the spread of the new arts and new philosophies would have been very much slower but for its invention. This was the impetus necessary to push civilization further out of the dark ages.

Some have it that the printing press was premature in that it provided a means for overproducing writing in relation to those who read. Possibly so, but any overproduction which did not occur could only have given a spur

to those who could not read. From then on, the growth of literacy and
the output of the printed word interacted with each other in an ever-increasing spiral so that, toward the end of the twentieth century, we are getting
very close (in advanced countries) to 100 percent literacy, with such an
abundance of print that almost everyone is reading at least something
every day.

From the sixteenth century to the beginning of the nineteenth century,
the growth was steady. During that time there were no major technical
advances in the printing press and its allied trades. All such advances were
by-products of the Industrial Revolution, which saw the mechanization
of production procedures and particularly the application of power. It
began in 1798 with the invention of a machine to manufacture paper,
and this was followed early in the next century by steam-driven presses.
Add to this the mechanical linotype and monotype methods of compos-
ing type and the application of photography for the preparation of illustrations, and the whole adds up to a tremendous surge forward in production, numbers, and costs.

It may well be that the nineteenth century was the zenith of print because the invention of photography and the harnessing of electrical power
together heralded a new era of communications. Still photography led to
moving pictures, which created the new mass medium of the cinema as
a kind of electronic extension of the theatre. The discovery of electricity
led to electronic communications by telephone, then audio broadcasting,
and then visual broadcasting, all challenging print as communication
channels. Broadcasting, particularly television, has such tremendous
power that it is not unjust to suggest that future historians might view
its emergence as equal to, if not greater than, Gutenberg's moveable type.

One further point should be made in completing this outline of the
communications of man.

Electronics has produced the computer, basically a counting machine
which operates in terms of "on" and "off" electrical signals and has forced
the invention of what could be the ultimate language, a language which
has been reduced to two symbols, "O" and "1," from which can be encoded
any other language. Speculation is rife as to what new frontiers of knowledge man may reach with his latest communicatory tool. Reaching the
moon would have been impossible without it.

It is into this record of development of communications that we must
fit the development of libraries.

NOTES

1. Marshall, J. D., "The Biology of Communication in Man and Animals" in Lyons, J., *New Horizons in Linguistics* (Penguin, 1971), pp. 229-241.
2. Gardner, R.A., and Gardiner, B. T. "Teaching Sign Language to a Chimpanzee," *Science* No. 3894 (1969), pp. 664-672.
3. Barber, C. L., *The Story of Language* (Pan, 1964), pp. 31-41.
4. Scholderer, V., *Johann Gutenberg: The Inventor of Printing* (British Museum, 1963), pp. 22-23.

Part Two

LIBRARIES
AS MEMORIES

4

Growth

The introductory chapters make it clear that the concept of libraries in terms of systems theory must be that they are systems specifically created for the communication of knowledge. The totality of libraries is theoretically an open system in that it is affected by the environment around it and in turn affects that environment. The environment is, of course, society, in particular the people of society who are responsible for the input and those who are affected, directly and indirectly, by the output. It is this interaction which makes a working library, but a prerequisite of this is that the library must store the data which may be required.

The analysis in Chapter 2 of the three communication systems shows that it is in the area of memory that the closest comparisons may be made. Man created his library system as a corporate memory of his society, and any judgment of the success of the development of libraries must include an account of how they have operated as memories, or data banks.

In terms of storage, libraries have been particularly successful as memories. While it has not yet been found possible to quantify in mathematical terms the total storage capacity of the human brain, it is patently much less efficient than even a two- or three-page document. This does not deny the power of the brain to select important and significant data according to its particular motivation at any one time, but such selection must be prejudiced by motivation, and at some future time the rejected data may be required for a different purpose. It is wise to store all data for possible future use, and this must be the basic purpose of libraries.

Consider the following:

In any case it is quite clear that man is a miserable component
as a communication system. He has a narrow band width, a
high noise level, is expensive to maintain, and sleeps eight hours
out of every twenty-four. Even though we cannot eliminate
him completely, it is certainly a wise practice to replace him
wherever we can. The kind of routine jobs that men like least
are just the kind that machines do best. Our society has already
made the first steps towards eliminating human bottlenecks
from communication systems and the years ahead are sure to
bring many more![1]

Librarians can claim that one of the first steps after the development
of writing and writing implements was the establishment of stores for
the products of the new technology. These go a very long way to eliminating the bottleneck of man's individual memory.

We have seen that, in general systems theory, growth is an important
example of behavior. Libraries, viewed as systems, provide an excellent
example of this phenomenon. The interaction of man and the knowledge
preserved for him in his libraries has led him to the re-creation of further
knowledge which he in turn records and feeds back to his library store.

Licklider[2] estimates that the total of alphanumerical characters contained in the world's literature is in the order of 10^{14}. Averaging a 200-
page book at 10^6 characters, we can estimate existing world literature
at some 100 million titles. In comparison, a mere 200,000 clay tablets
have been unearthed in the archaeological excavations of the Mesopotamian
towns inhabited by the Sumerians, Babylonians, and Assyrians of the
first four millennia B.C.[3] One of the largest of these early libraries was
the palace library of King Assurbanipal (668-626 B.C.) at Nineveh which
accumulated 30,000 clay tablets, a total which we may tentatively compare with the estimated 60 million items (15 million books and pamphlets) held by the Library of Congress in 1969.[4]

These statistical examples show, in a soulless fashion, the exponential
progress of libraries. They hide the essence of their growth as part and
parcel of the progress of civilization as reflected in libraries.

Whether the first libraries were in Mesopotamia or Egypt is still a
matter of some conjecture, but there is no doubt that the civilizations

which flourished there and achieved so much in the development of writing created many libraries for the purpose of storing the end products of their graphic communications. It mattered not that in Mesopotamia the end product was more often than not a clay tablet inscribed with cuneiform while in Egypt is was papyrus in the form of a roll on which was written the hieroglyphic script; in both instances the knowledge content was worth retaining.

These early libraries have been classified into four categories:

1. Temple collections
2. Government archives
3. Business records
4. Family or genealogical records[5]

This was the type of knowledge and data which early civilized man put into his memory bank, and basically it is what he has continued to add to. Here were philosophy and religion, science and technology, history and record. Literature, however, is more conspicuous by its absence than by its presence. That it existed, at least in the form of folktale, can hardly be doubted, yet there is a sad lack of its being recorded. It was the Greek and Roman eras which created and recorded the literary culture on which so much of Western civilization is founded.

The classical Greek era dates from the early fifth century B.C. It is Greek civilization that provided the most famous of all ancient libraries, a mirror which reflects its advanced culture.

The Alexandrian library was founded at the beginning of the third century B.C. and flourished for 200 years before beginning to decline. By 200 A.D. it was almost defunct, having had a more or less continuous history of some 500 years. By the end of the third century B.C., libraries were common throughout Greece, but it appears that by far the largest was that at Alexandria. Various estimates as to its total contents have been made, from 100,000 to 700,000 rolls, though the list produced by Callimachus totals only some 90,000 (but it is known that this excludes duplicates).[6] While the amount of writing on a particular roll obviously varied according to the length of the roll (they could run to some 150 ft.), the majority obviously contained more than the earlier clay tablets, which equaled about two or three pages of a modern book. When one adds to this the comparative abundance of other, albeit smaller, libraries throughout Greece, we have some proof of the growth of the system.

The Roman Empire, which succeeded and conquered Greece, continued the tradition of founding libraries, though it would appear that
there was some difference of purpose in that many were established as
spoils of war or symbols of affluence, while others were more soundly
viewed as repositories of knowledge and literature. The former is often
true of the collections of private individuals who, from c. 100 B.C., were
returning to Rome from foreign conquests and counted many books
among their loot, though later there is evidence that most Roman writers
and a number of professional men built up library collections. Titus
Pomponius Atticus, a book collector and book dealer, was reputed to
have some 20,000 rolls about the middle of the first century B.C. Some
200 years later, the writer Sammonicus Serenius accumulated some 60,000.
In the middle of the first century A.D. Seneca wrote that libraries were
as important to the wealthy as baths of hot and cold water.[7] The Alexandrian Library became part of the Roman Empire after Julius Caesar's,
conquest in 48 B.C. Indeed, some of its volumes became Caesar's, gifted
to him by the infatuated Cleopatra, who believed that she had the right
to give them away.[8] There is considerable speculation as to whether the
hasty departure of Caesar from Alexandria, resulting in the conflagration
of part of the city, caused damage or loss to the library, but it is certain
that in the next 300 years of Roman rule, the library suffered much damage due to the many uprisings against Roman domination.[9]

The fall of the Roman Empire saw the beginning of that period of
European history often referred to as the Dark Ages. From the fall to
the Italian Renaissance, there was comparatively little advance in civilization and this is reflected in library growth.

It should be added at this point that, in this general outline of library
growth, the omission of Far Eastern or, for that matter, Central and
South American history is deliberate. It has already been noted that the
failure of the East to evolve an alphabet severely inhibited progress, and
this is also true of the Central and South American Indian civilizations
which, in any case, were eradicated by the Spanish conquistadors of the
sixteenth century.

Throughout the Dark Ages only a spark of scholarship was kept alive,
and this was due to Christianity more than anything else. What interest
remained in learning tended to center in the monastic mode of life developed as a method of religious devotion. The main exception to this was

the beginning of universities as educational establishments, first at Salerno in the ninth century and later in the twelfth at Bologna, Paris, Oxford, and Cambridge.

The church's interest in preserving knowledge was mainly motivated by its own doctrines and dogmas. Any knowledge contrary to these was eschewed if not directly censored, but there were sufficient scholars within the church, particularly in monasteries, to see that the classics of previous eras were preserved. The many monasteries on Mount Athos, which had been ecclesiastical ground since Constantine moved from Rome to Constantinople in 330 A.D., eventually provided the Italian scholars of the Renaissance with many texts.[10] As perhaps could be expected the monastic libraries of Eastern Europe tended to concentrate on Greek manuscripts while those in the West, such as those at Monte Cassino, Tours, York, and St. Gall, were oriented toward Latin. Secular cathedrals and churches also had libraries and the total number was therefore large, but often in the case of the smaller churches the collection amounted to only a few devotional books. No medieval library ever reached the stature of the Alexandrian. It has been estimated that in Britain, the largest of the monastic libraries, those of the Benedictines at Bury St. Edmunds, and Canterbury, probably numbered 2,000 volumes, while the total in the country was no more that 100,000.[11] It should be noted that each volume contained two or three titles. This estimate is for the close of the fifteenth century, at a time when the growth rate of libraries was about to be drastically altered due to the invention of moveable type.

Whether the Renaissance provided the motivation necessary for a printing breakthrough or whether it was the breakthrough which accelerated the Renaissance is academic speculation of the chicken-and-egg type. What is important is that they did occur at convenient times to suit each other, and if there had been a Renaissance without moveable type, it would surely have had a very much slower growth rate. Overnight (in terms of the time spans we have been dealing with), the situation changed from one in which it was a most laborious human task to duplicate copies of a title to one in which many thousands of copies could be obtained with relative ease. The technology was in one sense too far advanced. It was capable of producing a very large number of copies for only a small percentage of literates. From then on, it became a prerequisite of a civilized country to increase literacy in its population so that

more and more people might gain access to the knowledge in print. How
far literacy increased depended on the social philosophies and material
affluence which were prevalent:

> I suppose one could venture to say that at the end of the six-
> teenth century the rate of illiteracy for the adult population in
> Western Europe was below 50% in the towns of the relatively
> more advanced areas and above 50% in all rural areas as well as
> in the towns of the backward areas. This is a frightfully vague
> statement, particularly because the terms "below" and "above"
> must be taken here in their broadest possible meaning, but the
> available evidence does not permit more precision.[12]

The statement is more vague in the present context because methods of
determining literacy for statistical purposes can only be at the level of whether
or not a person has the ability to read or to sign simple documents and
are therefore a poor guide to the ability of a person to make even an elementary use of books. It is safe to assume that considerably less than
50 percent could do this in the sixteenth century, and so in the succeeding 300 years, literacy has progressed to an over 90 percent level in advanced countries.

This advance has created an ever-widening market for books which
is reflected in the growth of libraries of all types. Taking a broad view,
the movement is one in which more and more libraries are established,
giving access to more and more people, albeit with different motives, cul-
minating in a public library system theoretically available to anyone but
used by only 25 percent of the population at any one time.

Libraries of private collectors existed throughout this time although,
in relation to the total picture, they have diminished in importance, many
of the best, by donation or sale, having become the nuclei of institutional
libraries. Possibly the largest collector in medieval times was Richard de
Bury, Bishop of Durham from 1333 to 1345, who was reputed to have
gathered some 1,500 volumes, although this is possibly exaggerated.[13]

The growth of institutional libraries has been relatively rapid and can
be outlined by concentrating on their development in Britain, since what
has happened there is reflected in other countries at a similar stage of advancement, including those in North America.

As early as the fifteenth century, there begins a series of libraries which were endowed by individuals, in the beginning mainly to schools and churches, but later to towns. The increase in their numbers is evidence of the growth rate. There were three in fifteenth-century England, the first in 1429, a gift willed to the citizens of London by Richard Whittington.[14]

Thomas Kelly, in *Early Public Libraries*, gives a checklist of endowed libraries in Britain from the Reformation to 1800.[15] This is a first attempt at such a list and it is almost certainly not complete, but it is satisfactory for our purpose. The list is arranged geographically and the dates of foundation given. From these dates the following can be ascertained.

Number of Endowed Libraries in Britain from the
Reformation to 1800 (i. e., 300 years)

Sixteenth century	13
Seventeenth century	83
Eighteenth century	163
	259

Most of these libraries were small. Kelly identifies those which had over 1,000 volumes (thirty-five out of the total).

A statistical comparison of this list with one of medieval collections of books is revealing. An appendix in E. A. Savage's *Old English Libraries* gives a checklist of collections from 778 to 1504 (a total of 700 years), of which there were 230.[16]

Almost all the endowed libraries ceased to function due to lack of upkeep, particularly financial. One outstanding exception worth noting is Chetham's Library in Manchester. Endowed in 1653 by Humphrey Chetham, it has had sufficient funds to survive to the present day. In 1684 its stock numbered 3,000 volumes; now it is in the order of 70,000.

The eighteenth century saw the establishment of other types of libraries besides those mentioned above. At the beginning of the century, two ministers of religion envisaged the possibility of setting up parochial libraries throughout Britain. The Reverend James Kirkwood of Roxburghshire presented a scheme to the General Assembly of the Church of Scotland which he set forth in a pamphlet entitled "An Overture for Founding and Maintaining of Bibliotecks in Every Paroch Throughout This Kingdom." This resulted in some nineteen presbytery and fifty-eight parochial libraries. In England, Dr. Thomas Bray, rector of Sheldon, Warwickshire, began a similar movement which was continued first by a group of trustees formed in 1705 and later by the Associates of Dr. Bray after 1730. By the end of the century, some 200 libraries had been formed, almost as many as the other endowed libraries in existence. Both of these movements were religiously motivated, and credit must be paid to the two visionaries and their helpers who began the formalized attempt to spread libraries throughout Britain.

Apart from these public-spirited ventures, the possibility of commercial profit from lending books was realized by booksellers. Beginning with the Circulating Library of Allan Ramsay in Edinburgh (1725), there was considerable growth in this field. By the end of the century there were around 1,000 lending libraries.[17]

A further series of private subscription libraries paralleled the development of the circulating libraries, beginning in 1741 with the rather unlikely example at Leadhills, Lanarkshire, which was sustained by miner's subscriptions. Most other such libraries tended to be organized by the middle class, or "gentlemen" of the time. Never so numerous as the circulating libraries, they maintained a high-quality stock of books. Despite the later development of free public libraries, some have had a continuous history to the present day. The most famous of the subscription libraries is the London Library founded in 1841 through the efforts of Thomas Carlyle and his friends. Today it too suffers from financial strictures, but because of its success throughout its history, it now has a stock of around 700,000 volumes.

Like the high-quality subscription libraries are the libraries of learned societies, the majority of which were established from 1750 onwards. Though they are individually small, the total of their stocks is large and of high quality.

The British Museum Library, which, in the course of its history, has taken on the role of the national reference library of the United Kingdom, was founded by an Act of Parliament in 1753. It began with the Sir Hans Sloane collection of 40,000 books and 12,000 manuscripts.[18] Its eventual objective, like that of other national libraries, is to collect and preserve the total output of the nation's literature, and the remarkable growth rate of their collections is evidence of the determination of society to have a collective memory of its graphic recordings. The British Museum Library now estimates its total holdings at 7 million volumes.[19] The American Library of Congress, founded in 1800, held only 3,000 works in 1814, when it was burned by British troops. At the present time, some 150 years later, it claims to hold 60 million items.

In theory, national libraries are available to all, but in practice, their geographical situations provide a severe limiting factor, and the nature of their collections makes them more valid for research workers rather than the average citizen. From the standpoint of a library service for the entire community, it is the emergence of the public tax-supported library movement which provides the best example of the memory growth.

The necessity for these libraries has its roots in the success, and sometimes failure, of the development of other libraries. In turn, the general continual growth of all libraries reflects the affluence of society, which, with continued technological progress, is capable of ever-increasing production of books and other graphics. Affluence leads to increased leisure time, and more time is then available for intellectual pursuits. Reading becomes more essential and this mothers the desire to acquire the skills of literacy.

In his book on literacy, Carlo Cipolla uses statistics of the growth of publications and libraries in the nineteenth century as proof of the growth of literacy. He notes particularly "spectacular developments" in the field of newspapers: "In the UK in 1831, the average monthly issue of the newspaper press amounted to 3,240,000 copies (= 137 copies per 1,000 population). By 1882 it had gone up to 135,000,000." [20]

It was perhaps natural that a new-found reading skill was turned in the first instance to the popular and sensational, but the amount of more serious literature also increased. A list of nineteenth-century best sellers shows that, on the sensational side, there were editions of some 2.5 million broadsides relating to murders in mid-century and, on the political side, a number of tracts reached editions of hundreds of thousands. [21] This was the golden age of the English novel and there are some revealing publications in this field. In the twenty years between 1829 and 1849, almost 79,000 sets of the Waverley novels were sold. From 1857 to 1863, some 140,000 copies of the *Pickwick Papers* were sold and 800,000 by 1879. On the practical side, Mrs. Beeton's *Book of Household Management* sold 60,000 copies in the first year of publication (1861), and by 1898, 640,000. These figures can be compared with the editions of the classics of around 1,000 copies published by the early sixteenth-century Venetian printer Aldus Manutius, who introduced to publishing the concept of scholarly but cheap books, necessitating the large edition compared with the early editions from the printing press of a few hundred copies.[22]

The ever-increasing growth is shown by comparison with some present-day figures. The New Testament edition of the Bible in 1961 by the Oxford and Cambridge University Press sold almost 4 million in its first year; *The Common Sense Book of Baby and Child Care* by Benjamin Spock sold 22 million between 1946 and 1969; the best-selling novel by Grace Metalious, *Peyton Place* (1956), sold 6 million in the first six weeks and 12 million by 1970; and the Penguin paperback edition of D. H. Lawrence's *Lady Chatterley's Lover* sold 3.6 million between 1960 and 1968.[23]

No doubt a considerable percentage of this flood of publications was of a sensational nature, but there was always room for the popularization of knowledge. A supreme example is the *Readers' Digest,* a periodical founded in the United States in the 1920s which has become an international institution—the layman's abstracting service—now selling at the rate of 29 million copies each month.[24]

It is against this background of technological achievement of production and increasing literacy that nineteenth- and twentieth-century libraries developed.

The Mechanics Institute movement was the immediate ancestor of tax-supported libraries. Born from the mechanic's classes of George Birkbeck, who in 1800 at the Glasgow Institute successfully pioneered adult education by organizing instruction for the workmen who made his apparatus, the first independent Institute was founded in Edinburgh in 1821. By 1851 some 700 had been established. Complementary to the basic purpose of verbal instruction were the libraries of the Institutes. The average number of volumes in each was around 1,000, the smallest having only a few hundred, the largest, Liverpool, 15,300.[25] Despite the fact that membership in these libraries was by subscription, many took pride in their working-class members. The success of the movement provided valuable evidence to the government committees of inquiry on public libraries in 1849 and 1850. The recommendations of these committees led to the presentation of a bill to Parliament, the essence of which was to allow local authorities of a population of over 10,000 to levy a limited rate of half a penny in the pound for the establishment of free libraries. The bill became an act on August 14, 1850, by the small majority of seventeen votes (118 voted for, 101 against). This substantial number against the bill reflects opinion against the concept of free, tax-supported libraries rather than an antilibrary lobby. This is substantiated by the fact that, once the principle was established, parliamentary opposition diminished and subsequent legislation was more easily passed. The first library to open to the public under the act was at Manchester, and in its first year it loaned 77,000 volumes. A further 60,000 were consulted in the reference department, a more than respectable total which gave hard statistical proof of the need for tax-supported libraries. This was accomplished from an initial stock of 16,000 reference books and 5,000 lending, which by the end of the first year had grown to 18,000 and 7,000, respectively. The population at that time was 308,000.[26] A present-day city of this population, Nottingham, has a stock of 541,000 and expects an annual issue of 3 million.[27]

Despite parliamentary success, considerable local opposition remained. Due to the permissive nature of the acts and the method of adopting them by public meeting and not by resolution of the local council, the growth of tax-supported libraries was not so fast as the idealists would have liked. By 1890 only 143 local governments had adopted the acts, although by the end of the century there had been a considerable expansion to the extent of 404 adoptions.

The increase in adoptions was due partly to subsequent legislation which made the process of adoption easier and partly to the considerable propaganda drive of Thomas Greenwood. Perhaps more than anything else, the financial benefactions of Andrew Carnegie, who personally gave some £1,750,000 and endowed the Carnegie United Kingdom Trust with a further £2,000,000, helped the movement. As an indication of the importance of this money, out ot seventy-nine burgh and parish libraries established in Scotland from 1853 to 1919, fifty-six benefited from Carnegie funds.[28] By far the majority of the adoptions were in urban areas, the spread of the movement to rural areas needing a special impetus. In the United Kingdom, the impetus was given by the Carnegie Trust, which in 1915 commissioned a report on library provision and policy. The report highlighted the fact that 43 percent of the population, mostly in rural areas, still had no access to public libraries.[29] This led to further legislation which encouraged the rural areas to adopt, and by 1950 there was total coverage. From that time, the propaganda for public libraries changed from the objective of complete coverage to that of implementation of standards of service, the achievement of which is the prime aim at the present day.

In approaching this outline of the growth of libraries from the stand-

point of the development of libraries freely available to all, it has, paradoxically perhaps, been necessary to by-pass the expansion of libraries
established in educational institutions. It might have been more natural
for a society to have established the principle of free education for all before that of free libraries for all, yet twenty years passed after the first
Public Library Act before the Education Act of 1870 made it compulsory for everyone to have a primary education. It is a very great tribute
to a large number of enthusiasts, particularly in religious movements,
that the general standard of literacy was sufficiently high for well-funded
libraries to have continued success. The main approach to education was
to teach the basic reading and arithmetical skills, and any advance made
on this was pedagogic. A heuristic approach to education was only dimly
perceived, and it is therefore no great surprise to find a singular lack of
libraries in all schools but the universities. The six ancient universities of
Oxford, Cambridge, St. Andrews, Glasgow, Aberdeen, and Edinburgh
had all established libraries early in their histories, though restrictions on
the use of their stock were often quite severe, Oxford in its early years
refusing to lend to undergraduates and also keeping books chained to the
shelves up to the end of the eighteenth century. The nineteenth century
saw the beginning of the expansion of the number of universities. The
total number during the academic year 1964-1965 was thirty, with a full-
time student population of 138,000 and a total book stock of some 20
million volumes.[30] By 1969-1970 this had increased to forty-five universities, 219,000 students, and 25,500,000 volumes.[31] The stocks of the
Oxford and Cambridge libraries are now in the region of 4 million each.[32]

     The growth of universities is only part of a general growth of educa-
tional institutions, and the number of colleges and schools is also increasing, although it is generally true to say that they pay less attention to their
libraries and that significant growth has occurred only in the post-1945
era. The establishment of a school did not necessarily mean the establishment of a library. A report on the education of 13- to 16-year-olds found:
"Of the schools in our sample only a quarter in 1961 had an adequate
library room . . . and more than another quarter had no library room
at all."[33]

     To some extent, estimates of the future growth of libraries must be
speculative, yet the perspective view of the history of their development
gives very sound clues as to what will almost certainly happen.

     It is estimated that around 1960, 39.3 percent of the world's population was still illiterate, a figure comparable with the illiteracy rate of six-teenth-century Western Europe.[34] As that part of the world has progressed since that time, so the rest will assuredly follow. It may be that differing political philosophies will start the progress along different lines, but the major trend is that the underdeveloped countries try to copy the more affluent, and there are certainly many examples of the creation of library systems similar to those developed in the West. A good example of this would be the West African country of Ghana. As the education systems of these countries eradicate illiteracy, there should emerge a mass read-ing public similar to that of the West at the beginning of the twentieth century. That many of them will turn to libraries seems indisputable.

The worst evidence of illiteracy, 88.2 percent, exists in East Africa.[35] The effect of this on libraries can be shown by taking one example. Mozambique (population 7 million) reports one national library (80,000 volumes), one university library (22,000 volumes), five school libraries (11,000 volumes), nineteen special libraries (115,000 volumes), and ten public libraries (51,000 volumes).[36]

In the East, China, with a population of 560 million, claims a public library stock of only 24 million.[37]

In prophesying the future of libraries in the underveloped countries, the only real guesswork is in estimating how long it will be before they reach the standards of the more advanced countries. That they will do so, given the economic growth which is necessary, seems inevitable.

It is equally inevitable that in the advanced countries, library systems must continue to grow, but the nature of the growth is worthy of a little speculation. That the amount of knowledge will increase is inherent in the feedback nature of the system.

If the estimate of 100 million titles currently available in the world is even only half accurate, it is clear that no library has all of them and, therefore, there are limits set by every library. The type of library which is most likely to have a very large collection is that which has as its objec-tive the preservation of stock for the purpose of historical and exhaustive research, that is, national and university libraries. National libraries, as the title implies, attempt to be exhaustive of their own nation's literature, al-most always collected by means of legal-deposit legislation. To this they add a selection of foreign literature which is most likely to be of value to the advanced research worker who makes use of their facilities. University libraries collect in the same way except that they will eschew many titles written at a popular and intermediate level, unless by chance they have also received the right of legal deposit.

Because of the exponential rise in publications, modern research libraries face considerable management problems. Most important of all is raising the necessary financial resources, which allow the purchase of sufficient stock, and the employment of the necessary number of staff to cope with the acquisition of stock and essential services to readers. The growth of stock also puts a heavy strain on storage, and much work has been done on compact methods of storage. In 1944 Fremont Rider saw the miniaturization of records as one of the major answers to the problem. He calculated that American research libraries were doubling in size every sixteen years and that this growth factor had been remarkably consistent throughout their history.[38] Most revealing are the figures for Yale University: a mere 1,000 volumes at the beginning of the eighteenth century had grown to 2.7 million by 1939 and will grow to a projected 200 million by the year 2040.

It is certainly not beyond the bounds of possibility that 200 million volumes could be stored in one library in their orginal physical state. On the basis that at least one library in a country should keep original copies of everything, it would seem that national libraries must face the problem of storing hundreds of millions of titles, but it would also seem uneconomic and unnecessary that this type of collection be duplicated within a country. Rider believed that the solution lay in the relatively new methods of microphotography, which are capable of reducing a 250-page book onto the back of a catalogue card, claiming that this effectively saved 100 percent of the space usually required since the catalogue card was needed anyway. Convincing as the argument is and despite further advances in microtechnology, there is no real evidence that Rider's thesis has become accepted practice. There has been an increase in the number of microforms stored, but they often add to or duplicate existing stock rather than replace it. The latest development is PCMI (Photo Chromatic Micro Image), a technique which is capable of reducing 3,000 pages to catalogue-card size. This does not make a significant difference in storage problems, but, in theory, "packaged" libraries can be prepared for a research worker who can then do his work at home, provided he has the necessary hardware to enlarge the miniature image to readable size. It is readers' resistance to doing just this that has hampered the fuller use of microforms. In a library, given the choice between a microform and the original, most readers will choose the original, but if their selected readings were already packaged in microform, they might choose differently. Only time will tell. Despite readers' resistance, it seems inevitable that many of the mangement problems created by the growth of research libraries should be ameliorated by the use of miniaturized records. Theoretically, it might be possible for national libraries to have miniaturized records of everything published throughout the world. The many countries which have established national libraries and given them legal-deposit rights are already in a position to produce miniaturized records, and it is just conceivable that an exchange system similar to that operated for government publications could be instigated. Copyright problems might prove the main stumbling block. In the present politically troubled world, it might be too idealistic to expect such cooperation, but some hope may lie in the United Nations Educational, Scientific, and Cultural Organization, which has been reasonably successful in a number of bibliographical ventures.

The problem could be very much reduced at a national level. If it is necessary for a number of research libraries to attempt to have exhaustive collections (and history would seem to suggest that it is), then it would probably be better to organize them in miniaturized form. The simplest way to do that would be to see that the miniature records were created at the source—the copyright office of a national library. Many libraries will still wish to have the originals, but it will be much easier to discard these at a future date with the knowledge that a miniaturized record is also held.

Unless there are considerable advances in computers as storage devices for library knowledge, it appears that miniaturized records hold out the most hope for solution of the storage problems created by continued growth. Licklider holds out some hope with the claim that the growth factor in technology is ten times that of knowledge.[39]

NOTES

1. Miller, G. A., *The Psychology of Communication* (Penguin, 1970), p. 55.
2. Licklider, J. C. R., *Libraries of the Future* (MIT Press, 1965), pp. 14-15.
3. Johnson, E. D., *History of Libraries in the Western World,* 2nd ed. (Scarecrow Press, 1970), p. 21.

4. U.S. Library of Congress, *Annual Report of the Librarian of Congress . . . 1969* (Library of Congress, 1970), p. 1.
5. Johnson. *History of Libraries,* p. 8.
6. Thompson, J. W., *Ancient Libraries* (Archon Books, 1962), p. 614.
7. Johnson, *History of Libraries,* p. 74.
8. Parsons, E. A., *The Alexandrian Library: The Glory of the Hellenic World* (American Elsevier Publishing Co., 1967), p. 284.
9. Ibid., Appendix to Ch. 15.
10. Savage, E. A., *Story of Libraries and Book-Collecting* (Routledge & Sons, 1908), Chs. 2 and 3.
11. Kelly, T., *Early Public Libraries* (Library Association, 1966), p. 15.
12. Cipolla, C. M., *Literacy and Development in the West* (Penguin, 1969), pp. 60-61.
13. Kelly, *Early Public Libraries,* pp. 26-27.
14. Irwin, R., *The Heritage of the English Library* (Allen & Unwin, 1964), p. 173.
15. Kelly, *Early Public Libraries,* Appendix 2, pp. 242-257.
16. Savage, E. A., *Old English Libraries* (Methuen, 1912), Appendix C., pp. 263-285.
17. Kelly, *Early Public Libraries,* p. 145.
18. Esdaile, A., *National Libraries of the World,* 2nd ed., rev. by F. J. Hill (Library Association, 1957) and Esdaile, A. *The British Museum Library* (Allen & Unwin, 1946).
19. Great Britain, Department of Education and Science, *Report of the National Libraries Committee* (Her Majesty's Stationery Office, 1969), p. 14.
20. Cipolla, *Literacy and Development in the West,* pp. 106-110.
21. Altick, R. D., *The English Common Reader* (University of Chicago, 1967), Appendix B, pp. 381-390.
22. Steinberg, S. H., *Five Hundred Years of Printing* (Penguin, 1955), p. 56.
23. *Guinness Book of Records,* 18th ed. (Guinness Superlatives Limited, 1971), pp. 92-93.
24. British Broadcasting Corporation, *Edition, 16 November 1973* (BBC 1 Television program).
25. Kelly, *Early Public Libraries,* pp. 229-230.
26. Credland, W. R., *The Manchester Public Free Libraries* (Public Free Libraries Committee, 1899), pp. 29-30.
27. Institute of Municipal Treasurers and Accountants, *Public Library Statistics, 1969/70* (IMTA, 1971), p. 12.
28. Aitken, W. R., *A History of the Public Library Movement in Scotland to 1955* (Scottish Library Association, 1971), Table 1, p. 349.
29. Adams, W. G. S., *A Report on Library Provision and Policy* (Neill & Co., 1915), p. 6.
30. Great Britain, University Grants Committee, *Report of the Committee on Libraries* (Her Majesty's Stationery Office, 1967), pp. 172-173.
31. Great Britain, Department of Education and Science, *Statistics of Education, 1969, Vol. 6, Universities* (Her Majesty's Stationery Office, 1971), p. viii.
32. Ibid., pp. 150-151.

33. Great Britain, Ministry of Education, *Half Our Future (Plowden Report)* (Her Majesty's Stationery Office, 1963), p. 14.
34. UNESCO, *Statistical Year Book, 1968* (United Nations, 1969), p. 30.
35. Ibid. p. 31.
36. Ibid., p. 392.
37. Ibid., p. 395.
38. Rider, F., *The Scholar and the Future of the Research Library* (Hadham Press, 1944), p. 3.
39. Licklider, *Libraries of the Future,* p. 20.

5

Preservation

The attempts of mankind to preserve his recorded communications could well be taken as a factor in estimating how successful he has been in coping with the human predicament. Evolved from animal stock, he continues throughout his history to display basic animal traits of acquiring territorial advantage over other species. His preeminent position over his environment allows his own species to multiply to such an extent that he is forced to seek territorial advantage over others of his own species or alternatively to cooperate to mutual advantage. There are many examples on both sides. He has tended to organize into larger and larger political units for cooperative purposes, and yet at each stage the units have continued to wage warfare against one another in an attempt to become supreme.

Libraries have grown in size and considerable attention has been paid to the preservation of the communications within them, yet they have constantly suffered from man's warlike activities. At the present day, the predicament is knife-edged in that technological advances have placed man in such a position that he is capable, with his nuclear armaments, of near-total destruction of his whole cultural heritage, including libraries.

A full history of the destruction of libraries has yet to be written— naturally so, since we are much more interested in what has survived— yet general histories of libraries abound with examples, major and minor. The loss of documents which could have been useful to future scholars is often lamented. This is particularly true of the manuscript era, the moveable-print era giving at least a statistically better chance of survival.

"When Ninevah was destroyed in 612 B.C. the invading Chaldeans and Medes apparently cared little for the clay tablets and simply destroyed the palace [of Assurbanipal] containing them by pushing in the walls with battering rams."[1] Thus fell one of the great examples of Mesopotamian culture, a fate which could have been worse since it was thus preserved for future excavations to rediscover. When records changed to papyrus, parchment, and paper, they were much more vulnerable.

The Alexandrian Library suffered many times and it is now pure conjecture as to what irretrievable losses were sustained. We have already noted the academic interest shown in attempting to determine the extent of losses which may have occurred due to the conflagration started by Julius Caesar when he burned the ships on leaving the city in 47 B.C.[2] Caesar probably took many volumes with him as spoils of war. It also seems probable that further burnings took place during the Islamic conquest, although (and this is proof of how scholars deprecate such losses) some Arab historians have attempted to vindicate the Moslems.[3]

The fall of the Western Roman Empire, conquered by the Goths, saw the further destruction of libraries. The Eastern Empire, founded at Constantinople in 328 A.D. was not to be spared its conflagrations. Fire, also, was a constant menace to manuscripts, especially in Constantinople where the dissatisfied populace often turned to direct political action in the form of incendiarism.[4] The imperial library apparently suffered the total loss of 120,000 volumes in the revolt of Basilacius in 477.[5] Between 727 and 843 further losses were sustained due to the activities of the iconoclastic emperors, whose destructions of idols often included books. Later, in the years 1203 and 1204, the city was burned three times by Christians on the Fourth Crusade, and this has been described as "possibly one of the greatest cultural devastations of the Middle Ages."[6] It is estimated that the losses at this time must have been enormous, and certainly much more than when the city finally fell to the Turks in 1453. The Turks are known to have sold many of the Greek manuscripts to the Italians, and these must have furnished textual sources for the early Italian scholar-printers.

Internal political struggles could also react against libraries. One of the best examples is the dissolution of the English monasteries by Henry VIII by his Acts of 1535 and 1539. Mostly, the books were dispersed, many being sold abroad, but some were saved for the king's library and others found their way to private collectors.[7]

Further revolutions and wars in modern times have also taken toll of stocks of libraries. In 1814 there is the example of the burning of the U.S. Library of Congress by British troops, a fate which, if it had happened during World War II, would have been catastrophic. That war saw the escalation of more or less indiscriminate aerial bombardments which greatly increased the possibility of damage and loss to libraries. Direct losses were suffered, but the surprise is that they were not greater. Russia probably suffered most, although libraries of Moscow and Leningrad escaped. The State University Library at Leningrad had removed most of its stock to Saralov. The King's Library of the British Museum was bombed, and at the repository at Colindale many newspaper files were lost. The central libraries at Plymouth and Coventry were lost, as was the lending library in Liverpool.[8] The total number of books lost in the United Kingdom during the war has been estimated at 20 million.[9] Immediately at the end of this war, the Inter-Allied Book Centre was set up as an agency for collecting and distributing stock to war-damaged libraries. When this work was taken over by the British National Book Centre in 1947, there was still a stock of 140,000 volumes to be allocated.[10] To some extent, therefore, stock was replenished and buildings, of course, were rebuilt, but the tragedy of irreplaceable records being lost was still a constant feature of the devastation.

One would have thought that in view of this lamentable yet apparently inevitable historical record, coupled with the threat of nuclear holocaust, the governments of the world would have been alerted to the necessity of taking special precautions to protect libraries, if only national reference libraries, from their certain destruction in a possible third world war. No serious plan has been advanced for this, not even for a store of miniaturized records. Some may say that this would be an action of pessimism, others one of realism. Whether pessimistic or realistic, such action has been taken by business organizations in North America. It is surely not vested interest which would make a librarian claim that the most important product of our civilization, our records of past achievements, must be saved for future use.

Libraries have also had to suffer the ravages of nature, although it has generally been easier to take precautions against this than against mankind's havoc. The volcanic eruption of Mount Vesuvius in 79 A.D. completely buried the Italian cities of Pompeii and Herculaneum and thus preserved certain aspects of Roman life for future excavations. Unfortunately, the majority of rolls which have been uncovered are illegible, the few which are legible only whetting the appetite for what might have been without the disaster.[11] A fire caused by lightning destroyed the Moslem library at Medina in 1257; the Royal Library at Brussels was damaged by fire in 1731; and likewise in 1851 the U.S. Library of Congress lost many of its 50,000 volumes in a second misfortune.[12]

Fire is obviously one of the greatest immediate dangers to libraries, but floods have also taken their toll. A modern example and possibly one of the worst in terms of loss of stock occurred in Italy in November 1966 when some 1.7 million books in the main libraries of Florence, Venice, and Grasseto were damaged.[13] One minor aspect of flooding is that damage has been caused by the water used in fire -fighting, an interesting example of the cure being just about as bad as the disease. Modern technology has provided a variety of fire-alarm systems, and one or another has been adopted by most libraries which take the preservation of stock seriously. It is possible also to have flood-warning systems.

There are other, more insidious dangers to stock, mostly due to poor-quality material on which the record is made or storage in adverse climatic conditions, but more often a combination of both. In the nineteenth century, the introduction of cheaper paper, mass-produced by mechanical means, led to a considerable reduction in quality. Even in libraries which took great care in preservation, a slow embrittlement of paper took place, resulting in books and newspapers which can be handled only with the greatest of care if the leaves are not to disintegrate. The basic problem is too great a level of acidity in the paper, either because it has been placed there in the manufacturing process or because it has been assimilated from the atmosphere. Preserving libraries now consider it essential to have a fully air-conditioned building from which the sulphurous elements in air have been removed. Considerable research has been done on paper manufacture, and it is claimed that it is possible to produce a paper cheaply which will still have lasting qualities. In a few instances, libraries may be able to purchase a copy of a title produced on lasting paper even though the bulk of the edition is on cheap paper. *The Times,* for instance, always prints a few copies of a "Royal Edition" on a rag-based paper.

It must be recognized, however, that the economy of the book trade dictates that the bulk of copies produced must be kept to a price to suit the individual rather than the institutional buyer. The paper-backed book, for instance, saves money not only in the cheapness of its binding but

also in the cheapness of its paper. This creates problems for the preserving library which has to collect them, and despite the fact that some of
them may have to attempt to keep the original for bibliographical purposes, reproducing the original in miniaturized microfilm can also be helpful. In the final analysis, it is the knowledge content which is paramount,
and if this is copied onto a base which has greater preservation proper-
ties than the original, then this is an advance. Microphotography invol-
ves chemical processing, and this must be carefully controlled to ensure
that no deleterious compounds remain. It is believed that this can be done.[14]

The theft of books can be serious enough from the library's point of
view, but is less serious than the complete destruction of the work. In
earlier times, it was common to chain manuscripts to their cases, a method
of making theft very difficult.

The psychology of fear was also used as a deterrent as this quotation
from a bookplate shows: "Whoever steals this book let him die the death:
let him be frizzled in a pan; may the falling sickness rage within him; may
he be broken on the wheel and be hanged."[15]

Even in the moveable-print era, chaining remained in a few instances.
Oxford University still continued the practice in the nineteenth century.

The tax-supported public library movement led, at the end of the nineteenth century, to open-access stocks which made pilfering relatively easy.
The advantages of open access are so great that despite continual losses,
libraries, except preserving ones, are most reluctant to return to closed
access. They have, therefore, used a variety of techniques to curtail losses,
and at the moment there seems to be some hope of a near-foolproof system provided by electrical technology. The principle of the system is that
each book is electronically "bugged." Each reader, when he leaves the
library, must pass an electronic eye. If he is removing a book illegally, the
eye is activated and a warning signal produced. What is happening is that
the electronic eye is taking the place of staff; all other methods relied on
one form or another of staff surveillance. To help this surveillance, control
points were introduced, sometimes with wicket gates, opened by the staff
when a reader was cleared. Readers were often asked to leave bags and
coats outside the control points, bookshelves were situated in radial fashion from the control point, mirrors were introduced to see inaccessible
points, and, as a last resort, floor walkers were employed to spy on potential thieves. All of these did little to deter the determined pilferer. It is
hoped that the electronic eye will succeed.

NOTES

1. Johnson, E. D., *History of Libraries in the Western World,* 2nd ed. (Scarecrow Press, 1970), pp. 25-26.
2. Parsons, E. A., *The Alexandrian Library: The Glory of the Hellenic World* (American Elsevier Publishing Co., 1967), Appendix to Ch. XIV.
3. Ibid., Appendix A, pp. 413-422.
4. Thompson, J. W., *The Medieval Library* (Hafner, 1967), p. 313.
5. Ibid., p. 313.
6. Ibid., p. 326.
7. Edwards, E., *Memoirs of Libraries* (Burt Franklin reprint of 1st publication, 1859), pp. 349-366.
8. Brown, J. D., *Manual of Library Economy,* 6th ed. (Grafton, 1949), pp. 15-16.
9. Johnson, *History of Libraries,* p. 227.
10. Allardyce, A., "The British National Book Centre," *Library Association Record* (November 1953), p. 344.
11. Edwards, *Memoirs of Libraries,* pp. 63-66.
12. Johnson, *History of Libraries,* passim.
13. Hamlin, A. T., "The Libraries of Florence, " *ALA Bulletin* (February 1967), pp. 141-150.
14. Kodak Ltd., *The Storage of Photographic Materials and Photographic Records* (Kodak Data Sheet RF-6), n.d.
15. Thompson *The Medieval Library,* p. 608.

6

Cooperation

No library has existed, does exist, or is ever likely to exist which completely assimilates all graphic records, and it follows therefore that from time to time a library will naturally turn to the stock of other libraries to attempt to satisfy a specific need of one of its readers.

In terms of systems theory, this would be regarded as amplification, a concept defined as "feedback due in any measure to the exploitation of local energy."[1] Taking a single library as a system, if it finds that its own memory bank is deficient for any reason, it will take steps to remedy the situation. Apart from acquiring new stock, the most obvious step is to make use of the stock of another library to amplify its own resources. Throughout the history of libraries, this has been done by a variety of methods, although it was not until the twentieth century that formalized schemes of cooperation were created.

The failure of any library to acquire a complete collection is more understandable, particularly if our estimate of a total of 100 million titles is anywhere near accurate. The administrative problems of obtaining, organizing, and storing this number are immense, and this figure does not include the nonbooks which would have to be included in a modern collection. In any case, the stock of a library is always geared to the needs of the readers it sets out to serve, and this almost always places limitations on the selection of material. Even in the case of national reference libraries, whose function it is to preserve all of a nation's literature, there are problems in complete coverage, particularly of the foreign materials which must be added to supplement the comprehensive collection of national literature because, naturally enough, advanced research work cannot be limited to the information produced in any one language. In addition, in terms of the history of graphic communications, the concept of a national library is relatively modern and the task of retrospectively gathering a comprehensive collection is an impossibility. Libraries also have often eschewed modern nonbook graphics, as we shall see in the next chapter. A Carnegie Trust report of 1924 states, "In general it is safe to say that, while individual libraries in many places arrange privately for mutual loans, systematic co-operation is yet in its infancy."[2] It is not at all difficult to substantiate this statement. It appears that libraries long ago found it necessary to supplement their own resources with those of other libraries. Elmer Johnson states: "inter-library lending was not unknown in the Middle Ages. Books were loaned to be copied and also just for reading."[3]

Johnson also quotes the example of the English library of the Priory of Henton which in one year (1343) loaned twenty volumes.[4]

A necessary adjunct to the interlending of books is a location system of some sort, and this was achieved to some extent by the production of catalogues. There are many examples of these, one source showing the production from the ninth to the twelfth centuries as follows:[5]

Ninth century	24 catalogues
Tenth century	17 catalogues
Eleventh century	30 catalogues
Twelfth century	62 catalogues

There was another estimate of 136 catalogues being produced in the twelfth century, after which there was apparently a decline.[6]

The first known example of a union catalogue, or a catalogue of a number of collections, is the *Registrum librorum Angliae,* compiled in the second half of the thirteenth century by that mobile and evangelical order, the Franciscans. The original manuscript is now in the Bodleian Library, but there are copies elsewhere. It covers the collections of 183 monasteries in Britain, listing works of ninety-four authors. The fact that this was produced is evidence of the need of these peripatetic scholars to locate works, and it is safe to assume that they were the means by which works were lent from one monastery to another.

At the beginning of the fifteenth century, a further union catalogue, based on the *Registrum,* was produced. It was edited by John Boston, who used the same enumeration of monasteries as in the *Registrum,* and added eight more, this time covering 673 authors. This work was entitled *Catalogus Scriptorum Ecclesiae.*[8]

From the fifteenth century onward, the considerable expansion of libraries due to the multiplication of books in the moveable-print era theoretically reduced the need for interloan and thus the need for union catalogues. The majority of large libraries continued to produce their own catalogues and since many of these were printed, copies found their way to other libraries; loans could then be arranged on an informal basis.

The growth of periodical literature emphasized the impossibility of any single library being definitive in its collections, and the need for a location tool was realized by the publication of union catalogues of periodical holdings of a number of libraries, sometimes of a particular type or group and usually of one country (although one publication covers the United States and Canada in true cooperative fashion). Not one of these publications is exhaustive in its coverage of titles, all tending to exclude publications deemed minor on a value/cost judgment.

It should, at least in theory, be much easier to be universal and comprehensive in the compilation of a bibliography, but even this has defeated the organizational powers of man in that he has always limited the scope of any work which he has attempted.

One of the first attempts was in the fifteenth century when, in 1545, Conrad Gesner produced his *Bibliotheca Universalis*. It listed some 12,000 items in Greek, Latin, and Hebrew, omitting vernacular works. There was one attempt at a supplement in 1548.

Late in the nineteenth century there was one apparently final but glorious failure to produce a universal bibliography. In 1892 Paul Otlet and Henri La Fontaine met. La Fontaine had been working on the documentation of material in the social sciences and, using this as a base, the two decided to create a comprehensive and universal card subject index. They soon realized that to do this, international bibliographical cooperation was necessary, and an international conference on bibilography was called in 1895. Subsequently, the International Institute of Bibliography was founded to compile a complete collected bibliography of intellectual literature. The Dewey Decimal Classification System was adopted for the subject arrangement but proved all too restrictive for the task. Its failure led to the creation of the Universal Decimal Classification, but other problems arose: "We see now that the first complete conception was altogether too vast . . . . Nor was it practicable then to collect within a single library, the colossal output of the printing presses of the world."[9]

Since then there have been no further attempts at universal bibliographies although a spark of hope has been rekindled by the application of computers to the task. The British National Bibliography, now the Bibliographical Services Division of the British Library, since 1950 has provided a current and cumulative coverage of United Kingdom printed works, although there are many exclusions, including many so-called minor government publications. The U.S. Library of Congress provides a similar service for American output, and cooperation between the two has resulted in the Machine Readable Cataloguing (MARC) project. The bibliographical citations and descriptions emanating from both agencies come in the form of computer-readable software which can be processed by computers to produce either comprehensive or selective lists. It may just be within the bounds of possibility that if all countries in the world produce similar software, a truly universal bibliography could result, but it could equally well be that this too is a concept "altogether too vast." One tremendous difficulty with such a project is that there must be a very high degree of standardization of bibliographical citation and a standard system of subject retrieval, and the situation regarding the latter has been described as chaotic.[10]

The whole situation could be altered if miniaturized records of all publications were originated at the source and a series of centralized depositories created so that all items listed in the bibliography could at least be obtained in microfilm. At the level of research work, this would seem to have very considerable advantages to counterbalance the disadvantage of having to use hardware to read the copy. Only then could we be reasonably certain of amplifying the resources of a particular library by a speedy service.

It would seem, in fact, that the trend in the organization of interloan services in the United Kingdom is aimed toward this principle. One of the most important recent developments in librarianship has been the establishment and ultimate success of the National Lending Library for Science and Technology (NLLST) (now the Lending Division of the British Library). Born in 1961 and fathered by the Lending Library Unit of the now defunct Department of Scientific and Industrial Research, it is one of the many examples of the very considerable resources that modern-day societies are prepared to make available in the pursuit of scientific and technological activities. At first, service was limited to the fields of science and technology, and works below the postgraduate level of treatment were not stocked. Later, its coverage was extended to the social sciences. In

1962 this library received 118,000 loan requests and by 1968 this had
risen by a factor of six to 716,000.[11] In 1971 it was confidently expected
that this would reach the 1 million mark.[12] The success rate for supply
of requests is around 90 percent, an excellent record, but it again gives
evidence of the difficulties of total comprehensiveness. About 4 percent
of the 90 percent was in fact supplied by two other libraries with which
the Lending Division has close links.[13]

Such is the success of this library that it now incorporates the National Central Library (NCL), another library in the United Kingdom which
has the interloan of books as its specific purpose. It was the NCL which
saw the beginnings of a formal scheme of interlibrary loans in the United
Kingdom. Founded in 1916 by the Carnegie United Kingdom Trust (after
the Adams report of 1915) initially to provide a direct loan service to
students who had no access to public libraries and to provide collections
of books for adult education classes, it was soon to become an interloan
library, lending books to libraries in response to requests from them. It
was this library more than any other which proved the necessity for the
amplification of stocks, and it is perhaps ironic that it should have been
taken over by the Lending Division. In its first year, it loaned 2,005
volumes. Despite the fact that it was not intended that it should lend to
other libraries, in its second year it had applications from three libraries,
and in its third year applications from ten. By 1922 it was lending
2,300 volumes to libraries out of a total interloan of 28,000; five years
later, the proportion had risen to 30,000 out of 45,000, and by 1934 to
53,000 out of 64,000.[14] In 1924 the Carnegie Trust reported that the
NCL was of supreme importance to students and that 160 libraries had
contributed about £190 in 1922-1923.[15]

By 1927 a government report recommended that the NCL should
become the main center for interloan between libraries of all types at
home and abroad, and by 1930 it had received government recognition,
changed its name to its present title, and received Treasury funds, thus
eventually becoming independent of Carnegie Trust support (from 1951).
Throughout its history it has continued to expand its services. It has
amassed some 2.5 million entries in various catalogues which aid in tracing
items not in stock; it has special arrangements with some 391 special libraries from which it borrows specialized stock; it created in 1948 a special
department, The British National Book Centre (BNBC), which arranges
exchanges of unwanted material between libraries; since 1962 it has had

the responsibility of maintaining and publishing the *British Union Catalogue of Periodicals*; it deals with some 1,500 bibliographical inquiries per year; it has accumulated a stock of some 450, 000 volumes; and it deals with 130,000 loan applications a year, of which about 78 percent are satisfied.[16] Despite this excellent record, it is clear from the success of the NLLST that the NCL has been very much biased toward the humanities and left untouched a very large demand for information in the sciences and technology. Table 2 shows how the NLLST loans were almost seven times those of the NCL and approximately 50 percent of the total estimate of 1,736,000 loans in Great Britain.[17]

Table 2
TOTAL INTERLIBRARY LOANS IN GREAT BRITAIN

	Reporting Year	*No. of Loans*	*%*	*Notes*
NCL	1969-1970	133,000	8	All loans and reproductions
NLLST	1970	890,000	51	Approximate
RLB	1969-1970	313,000	18	Including Scottish Central Library
Direct Loans	—	400,000	23	Very approximate
Total	—	1,736,000	100	

The NCL was originally situated in central London, mainly because of original Carnegie Trust financial help, but this site was considered costly for what is basically a closed-access storage library. Therefore, the British Library Act (1972) made provision for the federation of the British Museum Library, The National Reference Library of Science and Invention, The British National Bibliography, the NCL, and the NLLST into one administrative unit. The loan stocks of the NCL have been transferred to the NLLST site at Boston Spa in Yorkshire, thus creating the Lending Division of the British Library. As a factor in the unit cost of a loan, the respective costs of central accommodation have been estimated at £5/sq. ft. in central London, and £1.1/sq. ft. for Boston Spa.[18]

The amalgamation of these two libraries provides the United Kingdom with a central interloan library which will attempt to stock one copy of every "worthwhile UK publication together with a representation of important foreign material." In addition, it will probably "maintain a computer numerical list of British and American monographs in other libraries in the UK, to be published and distributed to libraries for direct interloan."[19]

It now remains to be seen what is to be the future of the Regional Library Bureaus (RLB). These bureaus are not libraries in that they hold no book stock except for bibliographies to help them trace material. They act as agencies for interloan by holding and compiling union catalogues of the stocks within their region. None of these union catalogues is entirely comprehensive and up-to-date, and they may be superseded by the computer numerical list, the present catalogues being used only for retrospective searching. Such a numerical list is already in successful operation in LASER (London and South-East Region). The cost to LASER has been estimated at £3,140 per annum, and to extend the coverage to all regions will possibly require £9,000 per annum. The cost of a computer print-out on microfilm which is up-dated frequently is £12 per annum.[20]

The subdivision of the United Kingdom into regions for the purpose of organizing interlibrary cooperation took place throughout the 1930s and was evidence of the success of the NCL and highlighted the need for amplification of resources. As can be seen from Table 2, their loan rate is triple that of the NCL, thus reducing the burden on the NCL and allowing it to concentrate on more esoteric requests. These regional schemes have provided further examples of attempts at comprehensiveness and the failure to achieve it totally.

A number of the regions established cooperative book-purchase schemes in an attempt to obtain a comprehensive collection of United Kingdom publications as cited in the British National Bibliography (BNB). All the schemes ran into difficulties, lack of financial resources being the major one, and when in 1959 the NCL announced that it expected each region to be self-sufficient, the regions, realizing the impossibility of this being achieved, decided to introduce a cooperative purchase scheme on a national basis.

The success of the Regional Library Bureaus led to a series of smaller local schemes being established, the first of these being at Sheffield (SINTO) in 1933. There are now probably about thirty of these in the United Kingdom, all operating a number of cooperative features—mainly the inter-lending of material, but also union lists of periodicals.[21] It is these schemes which generate many of the 400,000 estimated direct loans.

It is obvious that the growth rate of stocks of libraries is only keeping pace, if that, with the growth rate of publications as the introduction of formal or semiformal schemes of cooperation reveal the need for more and more interloan. If interloan of stock were not practiced, it would be very difficult to set limits of stock provision. The situation would appear to be exponential, in that the more stock a library provides the more interest in other stock is stimulated. While a glib answer to the question of the limits of stock provision is that there is none, it must be admitted that this is only a philosophical answer. If we look at the question from a management point of view, we must answer differently. At the moment, total coverage is an impossibility, even in fairly narrow subject areas. Financial and bibliographical problems of acquisition alone make this unfeasible.

There is, therefore, an optimum figure for the size of stock of a library, a figure which must relate very closely to the major objectives of the library and the financial resources made available. Cooperative interloan must be relied upon if libraries are to make available for their readers all the graphic resources of the world. It is to this ideal objective that all cooperative schemes, local, national, and international, have to be directed. How this ideal can be reached is a major management problem.

NOTES

1. Young, O. R., "A Survey of General Systems Theory," in *General Systems,* vol. 9 (Society for General Systems Research, 1964), p 73.
2. Carnegie United Kingdom Trust, *A Report on the Public Library System of Great Britain and Ireland (1921-1923),* ed. by J. M. Mitchell (CUKT, 1924), p. 36.
3. Johnson, E. D., *History of Libraries in the Western World,* 2nd ed. (Scarecrow Press, 1970), p. 122.
4. Ibid., p. 123.
5. Thompson, J. W., *The Medieval Library* (Hafner, 1967), p. 614.
6. Ibid., p. 614.
7. Savage, E. A., *Special Librarianship in General Libraries* (Grafton, 1939), pp. 285-293.
8. Ibid., pp. 298-310.
9. Bradford, S. C., *Documentation* (Crosby Lockwood, 1948), p. 97.
10. Wells, A. J., "U.K. MARC: An Introduction," in Jeffreys, A. E. and Wilson,

T. D., *U. K. MARC Project: Proceedings of the Seminar on the U. K. MARC Project* (Oriel Press, 1970), pp. 1-7.

11. Great Britain, Department of Education and Science, *Report of the National Libraries Committee (Dainton Report)* (Her Majesty's Stationery Office, 1969), p. 26.

12. Information received on a personal visit to the Lending Division of the British Library.

13. Great Britain, Department of Education and Science, *Report of the National Libraries Committee, p. 30.*

14. Pafford, J. H. P., *Library Co-operation in Europe* (Library Association, 1935), pp. 270-271.

15. Carnegie United Kingdom Trust, *A Report on the Public Library System,* pp. 40-41.

16. Great Britain, Department of Education and Science, *National Libraries Committee,* pp. 31-35.

17. Great Britain, Department of Education and Science, *The Scope for Automatic Data Processing in the British Library* (Her Majesty's Stationery Office, 1972), p. 377.

18. Great Britain, Department of Education and Science, *Report of the National Libraries Committee,* Appendix D, p. 313.

19. Great Britain, Department of Education and Science, *The Scope for Automatic Data Processing,* p. 63.

20. Ibid., p. 86.

21. *Encyclopedia of Library and Information Science,* vol. 5 (Marcel Dekker, 1971), p. 664.

Part Three

THE NATURE OF
THE STORE

7
Nonprint Items

Referring to the basic theme that man has created communication systems to complement his own, it is interesting to note that he knows much more about his own creations than he does of his own system. Psychologists are usually the first to admit that they have only an elementary understanding of how the brain and mind function, and the specific function of memory is one of the least understood. Pragmatic tests can show that one person has a better memory than another, a superficial analysis of how information is memorized can be shown (e.g., logical deduction, mnemonic devices, rote memory, eidetic memory), but the precise nature of the store is still not fully understood. If it were, we would surely be able to feed it more appropriately.

With man-made systems it is different. Because they are man-made, man understands much more clearly how they function; he knows that a computer is a counting machine using a simple binary code, and he manipulates this to his own ends in applying the computer to tasks with which his own brain has difficulty. Similarly, he knows that libraries are storage devices created to collect his recorded communications and he has a good understanding of how they should work. It was noted in the chapter on the growth of the memory that librarians must always be concerned with the problem of the best method of storing information. This problem can be looked at from different levels, two major ones being:

(a) What particular form of graphic is best for a particular purpose?

(b) How are these graphics best housed in libraries?

The second of these questions must be answered by the devising of techniques whereby stock is economically stored, displayed, and retrieved. The first is, generally speaking, beyond the control of librarians since

the vast majority of graphics are produced for an individual recipient; the
fact that they are very likely to be stored in libraries is very much a secondary consideration. For example, from time to time librarians, and
architects who design libraries for them, have suggested a standard book
size for ease of shelving in libraries, but what standardization has taken
place has been dictated by economics within the book trade, and even
these standards must frequently be set aside to suit a particular communicatory purpose of a work.

The simple fact is that if a library is viewed as a communications center
in the terms described, it has to accept whatever records are produced.
Any limitations which are introduced are dictated by the objectives of
the library, which, in turn, are defined by the readership. This limits only
the subject coverage and/or level of treatment. Any library which eschews
a particular form of graphic should only do so on these grounds.

This is not always the case and there are numerous instances of libraries regarding nonbook graphics as inferior. This has often been because
of difficulties in their management. The rejection of information and knowledge on this basis has limited the effectiveness of libraries as memories.
The use of the term "nonbook" gives the clue as to what has happened.

The word "book" nowadays refers to the physical record of a text
which is in the form of a codex; that is, the text is distributed to leaves
which are bound together. This is distinct from the ancient roll (*volumen*)
on which a text was presented, part by part, on one length of writing material which was then rolled up. The roll was particularly difficult from
the point of view of referring quickly to a particular part of the text, and
the codex was developed to overcome this. The Romans used wax tablets,
especially for letters, and when two of these were hinged together, they
were referred to as a *codex* ("a block of wood"), possibly because the
wax was held in wooden trays which, when they were closed, looked like
a block.[1] Sometimes two or three or more would be hinged together and
so the principle was established. By the first century A.D. the codex form
was in use for lengthy works, particularly in law, by the second century
some 3 percent of all books was in this form, and by the fourth century
it was preeminent.[2] It is a tremendous tribute to the Roman legal system
that, as a by-product, it produced the physical form of record which oust-
ed the roll, which had lasted for some 3,000 years, and has remained
preeminent for close to 2,000 years. If the Romans evolved the codex,
it was the Christian faith which adopted it and used it as the medium in

which it recorded its scriptures and doctrines, often with care, devotion, and painstaking artistry. Little wonder that these treasures, when stored in many medieval libraries, were chained to the bookcases for protection.[3] Little wonder too that any communication on any medium less worthy than the codex was regarded as ephemeral and eschewed by the libraries of the day.

Prior to the development of the codex, the two main media were the clay tablet and the volumen, or roll, the first developed by the cultures of the Mesopotamian valley, the second by the Egyptians. Evidence of the numbers of these which were produced has been given in a previous chapter. They were not the only media used, however, and some of the others also took their place in libraries.

Cylinder seals, rolled onto wet clay to make an impression were used in both Egypt and Babylonia. The mark made was most often a picture, occasionally with an inscription. The seals were used as marks of owner-ship and they do not figure prominently in libraries (unless we accept individual collections as private libraries).

Another method of communication, used particularly for public bul-letins, was to inscribe the message on a large stone or clay tablet. These are called stelae and were used by both early civilizations. They were placed where they could be seen by all, although no doubt most men had to have the message read to them. They can be regarded as the first news-papers, but since they were mainly single-copy editions, they were not viewed as library material. Today, many stelae from the ancient Near East, Greece, and Rome are housed in Museums.

An interesting example of ephemeral material is the archaeological evidence of the use of ostraca (pieces of stone and pottery) for the record-ing of bills, wages, letters, law suits, and other memoranda. "If not evi-dence of libraries, they represent the sources from which history is com-piled and libraries are eventually formed."[4] The ostraca often came from the homes of workmen.

Two other aspects of libraries deserve mention as contributory factors to the concept of the library as a communication center, although both are not normally considered as such. One is the tradition of placing sta-tuary in the library and the other is the decoration of the library. Ancient libraries provide evidence of both and the practice continues to the pre-sent day. It may be that the objective is purely aesthetic, but often there is a communicatory function.

The excavation of the palace library of Assurbanipal (seventh century B.C.) revealed that it had bas-reliefs of Dagon, the fish god, a fact which shows the strong connection of the library with religion.

Archaeological evidence of the physical nature of Egyptian libraries is scarce, but it is reasonable to suppose that they too had religious statuary since we know that they were mainly connected with the palace and the temple.

The library at Pergamon (second century B.C.) evidently had either portrait busts or portrait medallions of Herodotus, Alcaeus, and Homer since stones bearing inscriptions of these names were found in the excavations.[5] In the great hall, there was a statue of Athena on a marble pedestal, and a similar statue was in situ in the library at Ephesus.[6]

There is further evidence of statuary in the library of Prusa (first century A.D.), which had busts of Episteme (Knowledge), Arete (Virtue), and Sophia (Wisdom).[7] Hadrian's library at Athens (second century A.D.) contained statues of Homer, Sophocles, and others, and it seems to have been more a rule than an exception that in any library in Greece, a statue of Homer paid tribute to the founder of the Greeks' literary heritage, while libraries in Rome displayed a bust of Vergil.[8] In Roman libraries, the fashion of displaying busts of authors is attributed by Pliny, in the *Natural History,* to C. Asinius Pollio in 39 B.C., but it is obvious that the practice is much earlier than this.[9]

Attaching libraries to temples was still a common practice in Roman times. A temple built in Rome to the glory of Apollo and dedicated in 28 B.C. had two libraries, one for Latin and one for Greek, with a meeting hall in the middle containing a statue of Apollo and portrait reliefs of celebrated writers.

The excavation of a private library at Herculaneum gives evidence of the practice of placing the bust or medallion of an author in such a position that it acted as a symbolic guide to a particular section of stock:

> A small bust of Epicurus with his name in Greek characters, was found in the same room, and was possibly the ornament of that part of the library where the writings in favour of his principles were kept; and it may also be supposed that some other heads of philosophers found in the same room were placed with the same taste and propriety.[10]

Further evidence is shown in a letter of Eucherius, Bishop of Lyons in 441 A.D.:

> There were there [in a library] portraits of orators and also poets worked in mosaics, or in wax of different colours, or in plaster, and under each the master of the house had placed inscriptions noting their characteristics.[11]

The addition of the inscriptions adds weight to the communicatory function.

The library of Isiodore, Bishop of Seville, 600-636 A.D. contained stock in fourteen presses arranged and classified under portraits of the following:

1. Origen
2. Hilary
3. Ambrose
4. Augustine
5. Jerome
6. Chrysostom
7. Cyprian
8. Prudentius
9. Avitus, Juvencus, Sedulius
10. Eusebius, Orosius
11. Gregory
12. Leander
13. Theodosius, Paulus, Gaius
14. Cosmos, Damian, Hippocrates, Galen

It is extremely unlikely that the portraits were particularly accurate as guides.[12]

In the seventeenth century, one of Thomas Bodley's many gifts to Oxford University was a room which was intended as reserve space for the future; in fact, it was more than a century later that books were added. The room contained the Earl of Pembroke's statue, a painted ceiling, and a painted frieze of authors' heads. There is an illustration of this room in Hobson[13] showing it as it was in 1829. At some later date, the frieze was covered up due to alterations, but it was rediscovered in 1949 with considerable excitement.

The addition of portraits, busts, medallions, or pictures has been a major part of the overall ornamentation of libraries, but there were other forms of decoration. The Egyptian library at Edfu had texts and emblems painted on its walls. Some illustrated the instruments employed by the scribes. One wall was used to record the catalogue of hieratical books of the library.[14]

The Roman Emperor Hadrian (76-138 A.D.) established a "magnificent" library in Athens with spacious rooms "filled with paintings and statuary."[15] The paintings illustrated scenes from *Odyssey* and the *Iliad.*

The summit of library decoration was reached with the creation of a new library in the Vatican by Sixtus V in 1587.

> This noble hall . . . [is] probably the most splendid apartment ever assigned to library purposes . . . . In the decoration with which every portion of the walls and vault is covered, Roman methods are reproduced, but with a difference. The great writers of antiquity are conspicuous by their absence; but the development of the human race is commemorated by the presence of those to whom the invention of letters is traditionally ascribed; the walls are covered with frescoes representing the foundation of the great libraries which instructed the world, and the assemblies of the Councils which established the Church; the vaults record the benefits conferred on Rome by Sixtus V, in a series of historical views, one above each window; and over these again are stately figures each embodying some sacred abstraction—"Thrones, dominations, princedoms, virtues, powers"— with angels swinging censers and graceful nymphs and laughing satyrs—a strange combination of paganism and Christianity— amid wreaths of flowers, and arabesques twining round the groups and over every vacant space, partly framing, partly hiding, the heraldic devices which commemorate Sixtus and his family:—a web of lovely forms and brilliant colours, combined in an intricate and yet orderly confusion.[16]

An illustration of this library from a painting by Francesco Pannini in the later eighteenth century clearly shows that it is dominated by decoration.[17] The books are not be seen, being stored in cupboards on the walls and round six pillars which stand like sentries along the middle of the hall. Apart from some display cases, the only other tables hold decorative vases. No study places are provided; this is not a working library but a product of Renaissance art. As an outstanding, if exceptional, example of symbolic decoration, it is worthy of further study.[18]

The practice of including statuary and portraits in libraries has continued and can be seen in many present-day libraries, especially those founded
in the nineteenth century when ornate art tended to be in vogue.

One further type of decoration which can be said to have a communicatory function was the use of stained glass. This was introduced probably
about the ninth century A.D. for the religious purpose of creating visual
sermons for the illiterate but developed as a great art.[19] That often used
reading situation of the monks—the cloisters—also had stained glass.

The Peterborough Cathedral was:

adorned with glass of excellent painting; in the South Cloyster
was the History of the Old Testament; in the East Cloyster of
the New; in the North Cloyster the figures of successive Kings
from King Peada . . . . Every window had at the bottom the
explanation of the History thus in verse.[20]

There were further examples well into Victorian times, and many a
well-endowed Carnegie library had examples, despite the watchwords
chiseled on the stone outside—"Let there be light."

It was the metaphorical light of knowledge which was referred to, but
twentieth-century librarians demanded more and more natural light, and
stained glass is now anathema to modern library design. Ornate decoration has also disappeared, partly because of general trends in art but as
much because modern society is in a hurry and is also cost-conscious,
and ornateness is slow and costly. The adage that nature abhors a vacuum
still holds, however, and many a library wall has a designed wallpaper
and perhaps occasionally, in children's departments, this will have a communicatory motif. In some Scandinavian libraries there are painted murals which have been applied by artists subsidized to do so by brewery
firms. Photographic enlargements can now be made sufficiently big to
act as murals. One is to be found in the library of the new University of
Lancaster, where an early woodcut depiction of a printing press has been
enlarged and placed on a wall which is directly seen by all who enter the
library. Its symbolic decorative value is obvious; that it has communicatory value as well is clear, since so many questions were asked by readers that an explanatory leaflet had to be produced. There is some evidence

that libraries held certain other forms of communicatory media which were undoubtedly primarily intended as such but, because of the nature of their display, could also be viewed as part of the decoration. These include geographical globes, maps, celestial globes, and armillary spheres. Textual evidence of their existence in libraries is difficult to find, once again proving the point that writers concentrate on the book stock. For instance, Elmer Johnson's *History of Libraries in the Western World,* which is an extremely useful data source, contains no index entries for the above topics and no reference to them can be found in the text. However, this work is not illustrated, and it is from illustrations that examples of these media can be found. The camera captures all, even the autographic illustrations of libraries seem to attempt to depict faithfully all that they see with much less discrimination than a person who verbally or textually describes. Visual communication is sometimes superior to verbal.

Illustrations which show library decorations are perhaps best presented in tabular form, as is done in Table 3. Where possible, the approximate date of the illustration is given in the table.

The odd fact to appear out of this small listing of examples is the paucity of maps. The explanation is partly that globes were preferred, at least until printed maps were developed. The type of library in the sample also accounts for the small number of maps shown. The nineteenth-and twentieth-century public tax-supported libraries have made much more use of display maps, and it has been almost a conventional obligation that local maps and plans be given a prominent display position. There is a good example of this in Malmo Central Public Library, Sweden, although the particular method of display used there is only one of a number of possibilities.[21] From the early maps of the Egyptians and Mesopotamians, there was a very considerable growth of maps, both in technical quality and numbers, and very large numbers are stored in libraries.

The greater facility of the map has relegated the globe to a more decorative function, many examples occurring in children's libraries.

The lack of examples in this chapter may stimulate someone to undertake further research, but some doubt must be cast on the practical value of so doing. The simple fact is that, however important nonprint items have been in contributing to the library store, they have been swamped by the mass of works, not only printed but also in manuscript form. It is these that deserve more attention.

Table 3

EXAMPLES OF COMMUNICATORY DECORATION IN LIBRARIES

Type	Library and Date	Source*
GLOBES		
2 Globes with protractor, rule and cover, and 2 Globes, covered (on top of cupboard in an apparently inaccessible position)	Leyden University, 1610	(3) Endpapers
1 Free-standing globe beside a book-cupboard	Vatican Library, late eighteenth century	(3) pp. 82-83
4 Globes, free-standing	Austrian National Library	(3) p. 142
2 Globes (donated by Bodley, who possibly visited Leyden University)	Bodleian Library, 1675	(3) p. 168
5 Globes standing on floor, 2 others on table tops	Bibljoteka Jagiellonska, Cracow	(2) p. 304
2 Globes, free-standing in aisles between lecterns	Trinity Hall, Cambridge	(1) p. 37
2 Globes in aisle between stalls	Queen's College, Oxford, 1828	(1) p. 233
2 Globes, covered	Lincoln College, Oxford	(1) p. 251
MAPS		
Maps on wall	Trinity Hall, Cambridge	(1) p. 37
Framed maps mounted on walls	Leyden University, 1610	(3) Endpapers
CELESTIAL GLOBES AND ARMILLARY SPHERES		
Armillary sphere on top of cupboard	Vatican Library, Late eighteenth century	(3) pp. 82-83
Celestial globe by Vincenzo Coronelli	Royal Library, Brussels	(3) p. 101
Armillary sphere, free-standing	Library of the Royal Monastery, El Escorial	(3) p. 163

* *Numbers in parenthesis refer to:*
  (1) Streeter, Burnett H., *The Chained Library* (Macmillan, 1931).
  (2) Esdaile, Arundell, *World's Great Libraries: Famous Libraries* (Grafton, 1937).
  (3) Hobson, Anthony, *Great Libraries* (Wiedenfeld and Nicholson, 1970).

NOTES

1. Murray, J. A. H., and others, eds., *A New English Dictionary on Historical Principles* vol. 2 (Oxford University Press, 1884-1933), p. 582.
2. Roberts, C. H., "The Codex" in *Proceedings of British Academy, 1955* pp. 169 ff.
3. Streeter, B. H., *The Chained Library* (Macmillan, 1931), passim.
4. Johnson, E. D., *History of Libraries in the Western World,* 2nd ed. (Scarecrow Press, 1970), p. 39.
5. Clark, J. W., *Care of Books: An Essay on the Development of Libraries and Their Fittings from the Earliest Times to the 18th C.* (Cambridge University Press, 1901), p. 11.
6. Thompson, J. W., *Ancient Libraries* (Archon Books, 1962), p. 84.
7. Ibid., p. 85.
8. Ibid., p. 85.
9. Clark, *Care of Books,* p. 12.
10. Ibid., p. 24.
11. Ibid., p. 43.
12. Ibid., p. 45.
13. Hobson, A., *Great Libraries* (Weidenfeld and Nicholson, 1970), p. 173.
14. Thompson, *Ancient Libraries,* pp. 3-4
15. Johnson, *History of Libraries,* p. 72.
16. Clark, *Care of Books,* pp. 47-48.
17. Hobson, *Great Libraries,* pp. 82-83.
18. Clark, *Care of Books,* Fig. 18.
19. On this subject, see *Encyclopaedia Britannica* vol. 21 (1947), pp. 291-296.
20. Quoted in Clark, J. W., *Care of Books,* p. 100 from Gunton, S., "History of the Church of Peterborough" (1686).
21. Orr, J. M., *Designing Library Buildings for Activity* (Deutsch, 1972), Pl. 11.

8
Archives

The preeminent position of the book as the main medium to be stored
has been particularly true of the institutional library where the archival
or more ephemeral material was often ignored. More often than not, the
collection of this type of material was left to the individual private library,
although very often, when this was later dispersed, the entire contents became the property of an institutional library. In the following examination of nonbook items in libraries, a number of examples of this aspect of
collections will be noted. This suggests that the institutional library was
rather narrow in its thinking as to what it should store, or alternatively
(and this is more likely in many cases) that this type of library lacked the
staff to cope properly with the nonbook and the management problems
it introduced, whereas an individual was prepared to spend time organizing
this "fugitive" material because of the special interest it held for him.
The fact that the institutional library is later only too happy to welcome
private collections to its store only shows that it should have been collecting it in the first place.

Taking an overall view of libraries rather than a narrow view of one particular type, it is quite clear that they have always collected all media, no
matter what type mankind chose to record.

After the evolution of the codex and its adoption by Christian scribes,
by far the majority of records were created in this form. Earnest Savage
provides a most interesting checklist of medieval collections between the
years 778 and 1504. Out of the 230 collections listed, only in four examples can evidence be found of the nonbook. Such is their scarcity that it

is probably worth listing them and noting that in three instances they belong to individuals:

1. In 1150 Hugh of Leicester donated to Lincoln Cathedral 42 vols. and *Map of World.*
2. In 1443 John Brette, student at Oxford, owned one book . . . and a *pamphlet.*
3. In 1457 Dr. Thomas Gascoigne, Chancellor of Oxford left books and *quires* written on paper to Syon Monastery.
4. In 1504 the classification of volumes in Syon Monastery contained a class for *Devotional Tracts.* (It is highly likely that these were bound in book form).[1]

The difficulty with such evidence is that it ignores archival collections, both public and private. These consisted mainly of letters, legal documents, and accounts, and their physical format was mainly the broadsheet or alternatively the roll which was often used for the more formal charter which was still produced on parchment. It is estimated that there were more than a thousand such charters from the early kings of England before the Norman conquest.[2] It is not until 1199 that the Lord High Chancellor began to keep duplicate copies; later he acquired a special clerk to keep the records who later assumed the title "Master of the Rolls," giving the clue to the formats he was in charge of.[3] The growth of officialdom in the form of church and state records is well illustrated from this time on by the increase in their records and by the fact that in 1838 the Public Record Office was formed in London as a centralized depository: "Huge quantities of records, often unsorted, uncatalogued, and even unlabelled were brought to Chancery Lane."[4] Since that date, many more record offices have been established at the local level, the first in Bedford in 1923.[5] Many of these have collected family records; for example, the Lincolnshire Archives Committee has the records of some seventy families which had to register their estates after the first Jacobite Rebellion of 1715.[6]

There is no clear-cut demarcation line between an archival collection and a library collection. A good guide might be taken from the following:

A document which may be said to belong to the class of Archives is one which was drawn up or used in the course of an administrative or executive transaction (whether public or private) of which itself formed a part; and subsequently preserved in their own custody for their own information by the person or persons responsible for that transaction and their legitimate successors.[7]

or alternatively:

Thus behind the facade of old leather bound books and underneath the lids of cardboard boxes lie masses of information written by earlier generations, not for posterity, but in the course of their official and private lives.[8]

The words "not for posterity" seem to provide the distinction, but the judgment as to what is or is not for posterity is often hard to make. However, it does explain why archival material is not often in the more permanent codex format. Even when one is quite clear as to what is archival as distinct from library material, it is soon discovered that the use of one leads to the other, and one is reminded that the similarities of the information contained in the different documents are stronger than any dissimilarity in intent or in format. The Greater London Record Office has a special collection of maps and prints and also a photographic library of some 14,600 photographs.[9] Examples of similar collections in libraries will be cited later. There are also examples of records of libraries, such as catalogues, registers of laws, rules and regulations, and committee minutes, which have found their way to record offices.[10]

An interesting example of how modern society pays more attention to its archival ephemera is the BBC Written Archives Centre at Reading. Formed in 1922, the BBC realizes how important a role it has played in modern society and how its records are of considerable importance to historians. As with a great deal of official and semiofficial records, these records are released only after a certain length of time. (At the moment, only documents before 1954 are available, but the date is advanced every so often.) They have been the source material for Asa Briggs's *History of Broadcasting in the United Kingdom.*[11] This archival collection, as others, abounds with nonbooks. There are scripts, correspondence, minutes of meetings, memoranda, program details, press cuttings, and BBC booklet and pamphlet publications. There are many examples of archival material stored in modern conventional libraries, a situation which further confuses

the distinction between the two and leads to the conclusion that they
are basically the same. Most national libraries have some archival collections. The British Library, Reference Division, has in its Department of
Manuscripts some 100,000 charters and rolls.[12] A much smaller collection
of "charters, deeds and similar documents" is held by the John Rylands
Library in Manchester. The catalogue of these documents notes only
those of which the provenance has been established and contains, among
others, some of the Beaumont charters, the earlier part of the collection
of Abbé de la Rue, a Norman scholar, a section of papers of Sir Edward
Nicholas, Secretary of State to Charles I and II, papal bulls and briefs relating to the Medici family, and a collection of charters of Sir Thomas
Phillipps.[13] In the preface to the catalogue, a plea is made for more collections to be donated.

At the risk of appearing to go from the sublime to the ridiculous, the
following is an isolated example of a collection of archival material which
was brought together by an individual and later donated to an institutional library. In the Mitchell Library, Glasgow, there is a ten-volume
set of programs of meetings and entertainments held in the City Hall from
1865 to 1885. These were donated by Mr. Duncan Brown, who was the
hall keeper.[14]

What is obvious, even from this short account, is that archival material is part of the institutional memory store, whether it be called a records office or a library. It would appear that libraries avoided collecting
archives, only to find that they were to be given them by way of donation,
and that while the bulk of archives is now in records offices, libraries do
store some.

In the case of autographs and holographs, the demarcation line between
what is an archive and what is not is often blurred. Much archival material
is in manuscript form, and much of this in letter form although, strictly,
the subject of the letter should be that of a transaction, legal or otherwise.
As the affluence of man allowed him more time to investigate his history,
there was more and more demand for source material and the collections
grew. As literacy grew, so did the volume of correspondence. If letters
were written by persons of historical significance, they too became important. In the field of literature, more and more detailed criticism led to a
demand for authors' original manuscripts, and it has become important
to keep these. The major collections of autographs and holographs of historical and literary figures seem to be in libraries rather than in record offices.

In searching for examples, I have looked at some of the great preserving libraries, national and academic, but I have also made considerable use of Thomas Mason's *Public and Private Libraries of Glasgow,* a work which provides numerous examples of such material in private collections at the end of the nineteenth century.[15] These examples reflect the nature of such collections in similar libraries throughout the United Kingdom and in other similar countries throughout the world.

In 1736 the Bodleian received a donation from an antiquary, Thomas Tanner, which included a large series of letters of English Civil War Times.[16] The Universitatsbibliothek in Leipzig has a collection of 20,000 letters and autographs bequeathed in 1892 by Georg Kestrer, and this is part of a total collection of 90,000.[17] The Biblioteca Ambrosiana, Milan, received in 1928 the Bonomelli collection of letters, which mainly relate to the Italian Risorgimento.[18] The Ford collection in the New York Public Library of 60,000 items is mainly of autographs of famous Americans who lived before the American Civil War.[19]

The sample of libraries in Glasgow provides excellent examples of this type of collecting. The library of Bernard MacGeorge had an album of holographs, including an attributed poem, "Dolorida," by Swinburne; a poem by Longfellow; and contributions from Dickens, Dumas *père,* and Charles Reade.[20] The library also had several autographs of the Paisley poets. In 1883 there was added to the Mitchell Library a collection of autographs and printed papers formed by James Gould of Edinburgh, who in 1859, the year of Robert Burns's centenary celebrations, obtained all the signatures of Burns's descendants and living relatives, together with the signatures of his leading admirers in all parts of Scotland.[21] The Mitchell Library also has letters of acceptance or apology from those who were invited to the main celebration. These include Lord Brougham, Thomas Carlyle, Dickens, Tennyson, and Thackeray.[22] The Euing Music Library is accredited with "a number of manuscript works including autographs of great musicians, etc."[23] The most remarkable collection is that of James Guild, whose library held some 400 letters, each in a brown envelope, classified in fifteen portfolios. The literary portion is the largest and includes Scott, Burns, Byron, Shelley, Dickens, and Thackeray; but history is also represented in George II and III, Louis XIV, Pitt, Fox, and Peel; and the theatre in Irving and Terry.[24] Regretfully, this fine collection was not donated to an institutional library but sold by auction in 1888. A paper clipping (almost certainly from the *Glasgow Herald*) in the Mitchell

Library records that the largest audiences turned up for the sale of autographs. It seems that many of the prize items were sold singly, one by Mary, Queen of Scots, fetching £14.10s, one by Burns, £11, and one by George Washington £8.5s. At the sale of books, a Kilmarnock edition of Burns was bought for the John Rylands Library for £260.

To conclude, here is a quotation from an essay by Asa Briggs on the Department of Manuscripts in the British Library, Reference Division:

> There are few professional historians in Britain—or post-graduate students working on historical topics—who have not paid at least one visit to the Manuscripts Department of the British Museum. There are many historians, indeed, who go there as often as they can, armed with notebooks and a plentiful supply of sharp pencils. To them, the British Museum, like the Public Record Office in Chancery Lane, is a workshop, and the noise of 20th Century London is shut out as they return through their studies not only to historic London but to the whole of the lost world of the past.[25]

NOTES

1. Savage, E. A., *Old English Libraries: The Making, Collection and Use of Books During the Middle Ages* (Methuen, 1911), Appendix C, pp. 263-285.
2. Galbraith, V. H., *An Introduction to the Use of Public Records* (Oxford University Press, 1934), p. 16.
3. Ibid., p. 3.
4. Ibid., p. 5.
5. Landau, T., *Encyclopedia of Librarianship,* 2nd ed. (Bowes and Bowes, 1961), p. 22.
6. Lincolnshire Archives Committee, *Archivists' Report 9* (1958), pp. 6-7.
7. Jenkinson, H., *Manual of Archive Administration,* 2nd rev. ed. (Lund Humphries, 1965), p. 11.
8. Green, R. J., *York City Archives, St. Leonard's Papers No. 1* (York Public Libraries, 1971), p. 15.
9. Greater London Record Office and Library, *Report, 1971* (Greater London Council), p. 17.
10. "Library History in Archives" in *Library History* (Autumn 1972), pp. 250-252.
11. Briggs, A., *History of Broadcasting in the United Kingdom* (Oxford University Press, 1961).
12. *Libraries, Museums and Art Galleries Year Book, 1971* (J. Clarke & Co., 1971), p. 321.

13. Fawtier, R., *Hand-List of Charters, Deeds and Similar Documents in the Possession of John Rylands Library* (Manchester, The University Press, 1925), p. vi.

14. Mason, T., *Public and Private Libraries of Glasgow* (T. D. Morison, 1885), p. 146.

15. Ibid.

16. Esdaile, A., *Famous Libraries of the World* (Grafton, 1934), p. 10.

17. Ibid., pp. 213-214.

18. Ibid., p. 256.

19. Ibid., p. 423.

20. Mason *Public and Private Libraries of Glasgow,* pp. 303-304.

21. Ibid., p. 128.

22. Ibid., p. 135.

23. Ibid., p. 192.

24. Ibid., pp. 258-262.

25. *Treasures of the British Museum* (Collins, 1971), p. 170.

9

The Moveable Print Era

If medieval libraries avoided the nonbook, considering it ephemeral, they established a tradition of libraries as storage depots for books which some hold is still very much with us, despite an abundance of evidence that the nonbook has also been stored. This evidence shows that the principle that the nonbook is part of the store has been conceded, and it is only the degree to which it is given prominence which is controversial.

That epoch-making event, the invention of moveable type in the 1450s, had, as its main effect, the increase in the number of books available, but it also made possible the multiplication of lesser works in the form of broadsheets, leaflets, pamphlets, and periodical literature, all of which have found their way into libraries in ever-increasing numbers. Indeed, despite the importance given to the Gutenberg Bible of 1456 as the first printed book, it was predated by a year by at least two printed broadsheets in the form of indulgences, and common sense suggests that much of the experimentation with the new technology was with broadsheets rather than full-length works.[1] The fact that the first book was a Bible is a tribute to the influence of Christianity, which elevated that book to its position as the world's best seller. Prior to moveable print, many broadsheets were printed by wood block, but few examples remain extant. One of the most famous, because it is dated 1423, is the "St. Christopher" print of which there is only one extant copy, a treasured possession of the John Rylands Library.[2]

The term "broadsheet" is used here in its bibliographical sense, describing the physical form of an unfolded (at least in its original state) sheet of material, thus distinguishing it from the leaflet, which is folded but unstiched, and the pamphlet, which is folded and stitched (or pseudostitched).

Such bibliographical distinctions are useful for descriptive purposes and therefore provide a relatively useful classification for the survey of this part of a library store. The terminology is often used loosely, however, and demarcation lines are sometimes difficult to draw. For instance, the distinction between a leaflet and a pamphlet is a subtle one and not of great practical consequence. For that matter, few people would think of a newspaper as a leaflet, and in such a case it is obviously better to use the specific term rather than the somewhat forced generic one.

Almost certainly the most prevalent type of broadsheet in libraries is the sheet map. The British Library, Reference Division, has a stock of 1,050,000 sheets, surpassed only by its collection of 4 million postage stamps. The latter is a specialized collection and few other libraries have any, whereas sheet maps are commonplace.[3] Another large collection in the United Kingdom is that held by the Royal Geographical Society, totaling some 500,000, which complements the British Library, Reference Division collection in that it concentrates more on modern maps.[4] The United States Library of Congress holds some 3,270,000 maps, statistically one of its largest collections.[5] It is safe to conjecture that a library of any type will at least stock maps and plans of local interest.

Drawings (originals) and prints (duplications of drawings) are also present in large numbers in library stores, although there is some conflict here between the role of the library and the role of the art gallery. It is obvious that both are centers for the collection of various forms of graphic communication and that the division between the two is more an administrative convenience, and thus there is a lack of a clear-cut demarcation line. If anything, that line is drawn between prints and originals, the latter clearly the province of the art gallery although in many instances they will be found in modern libraries. It is true that the picture-lending schemes of the modern public library mostly stock prints of original paintings, but there are a few which actually lend originals (mostly of local artists). There are many examples of this in London public libraries.[6] In any case, let us remember that many early libraries, such as the Alexandrian, were established as museums and libraries. The administrative separation of the two and the addition of the third institution, the art gallery, is a modern development which only adds evidence to the fact that the increasing complexity of communications centers apparently necessitates some kind of administrative separation. A further example of this is shown in the administration of the prints and drawings collected in the British Museum. This has the status of a separate department, created in 1808 apparently because there had been difficulties with a caricaturist, Robert Dighton, who had systematically been stealing prints.[7] This department now contains many hundreds of thousands of items and it is claimed that the collection is based on the principles of connoisseurship.[8] As a further example of the importance of the Museum's collections and how they have attracted further donations, the bequest of Turner's studio contents of some 19,000 items may be cited.[9] The department till 1808 was part of the Museum, then was transferred to the library, and under the recent organization of the British Library reverted back to the Museum.

An example of a specialized collection of drawings is that of the Royal Institute of British Architects, where 250,000 items are held, representing work from the sixteenth century to the present.

Prints (as the name implies) developed parallel to moveable-print. Printing from wood blocks developed from the practice of printing on textiles and possibly had its roots in the early practice of impressing seals. The printing of playing cards is known to have occurred in Germany in the late fourteenth century, and in the fifteenth century the years between 1430 and 1450 saw the production of "block books," a practice which continued for some time in the fifteenth century after Gutenberg's invention.[10] Moveable type, however, was obviously the tool for textual matter. Printing from a block was therefore almost totally confined to illustrative material and developed into a high art form, particularly with the introduction of the finer-lined methods of engraving, etching on metal, and later wood engraving (as opposed to woodcut).

Prints, and occasionally drawings, are to be found in our sample of libraries as follows:

1. New York Public Library: A print room founded in 1899 now houses 100,000 prints.[11]

2. Guildhall Library, London: Collections of over 40,000 prints.[12]

3. Bodleian Library, Oxford: A bequest by Richard Gough in 1809 included maps and prints. The Douce collection added in 1820 included a large number of prints and drawings.[13]

4. Bibliothèque du Museum National d'Histoire Naturelle, Paris: in 1933 it held a collection of 19,500 original drawings, including vellum paintings. These paintings are of rare plants in the garden

of Gaston, Duke of Orleans and also the Royal Garden of Louis
XIV. They were originally kept at the Bibliotheque Royale, but
transferred to this library in 1794. It should be noted that this is
the library of a museum.[14]

5. (a) MacGeorge Library: Complete collection of twenty etchings of
Charles Meryon.

(b) Shield Library: Twenty-five views of Glasgow 1693-1853.

(c) Guild Library: 315 separate portraits of Mary, Queen of Scots,
and also a miscellaneous collection of portraits of Mary's reign,
including eighty of Shakespeare and sixty of Walter Scott.

(d) Gray Library: Ninety-two portraits of Mary, Queen of Scots.[15]

The fine-art print is only one form of printed broadsheet; there are numerous examples of others collected by libraries, some being difficult to
view as communications of knowledge. But the fact that they are collected
shows the difficulty of drawing a line and the natural tendency of a library
to be a collector and preserver.

As an adjunct to the theatre and its history, playbills are to be found often in the local-history collections of public libraries. A fine general collection is to be found in the Huntington Library, California. A private collector's library, it acquired in 1914 the Kemble-Devonshire collection of plays,
part of which consists of 111 volumes of playbills of the period from 1750
to 1787.[16] In the United Kingdom, Leeds Public Library has a collection
of 1,500 playbills, and Finsbury Public Library a special collection relating to the Sadler Wells Opera Company.[17]

Apart from the specific purpose of advertising the production of a play,
handbills and posters were produced for a variety of other reasons. In
introducing examples of these, it might be best to begin with a historical
one to remind us that the broadsheet, poster, or proclamation is anything
but new. The library of the monastery of St. John at Patmos has a series
of framed broadsheets on its walls, a particular specimen being a golden
bull of Emperor Alexius Comnenus of 1088.[18]

One important collection of proclamations, placards, and other broadsheets and bulletins is at the John Rylands Library, Manchester. A gift
to the Library by the Earl of Crawford and Balcarres, it contains 20,000
items issued in France and other countries.[19]

The use of posters connected with war is shown in the collection of

16,000 at La Bibliothèque et Musée de la Guerre, Paris.[20]

The simplicity and economy of the printed broadsheet are shown in its production by clandestine and secret presses. A special collection of works on Italian history at Harvard contains some 5,000 broadsheets, most of them from such presses.[21]

At the Huntington, as part of the Britwell Court Library, there are a number of broadsheet ballads which illustrate the use of this medium in disseminating the words of the popular songs of the day.[22]

In George Gray's private library in Glasgow were some 1,000 broadsheets of proclamations, executions, dying speeches, and other subjects relating to Covenanting times.[23] A similar collection of 500 resides in the Alexander MacDonald Library, those of executions relating particularly to the Glasgow area.[24]

Finally, so far as broadsheets are concerned, mention should be made of the habit of collecting bookplates, a communicatory medium far removed from the printed book itself but very much a collector's item. The following examples once again show how often the private collection finds its way to the institutional library.

In 1897 the British Museum was gifted with a large collection of bookplates by A. N. Frank: they are in the Department of Prints and Drawings and so they were obviously viewed as specimens of fine art. Another collection of 8,000 was added in 1950 with a donation by G. H. Viner. The Universitatsbibliothek, Leipzig, has an ex-libris collection of about 10,000, and the Herzog August Bibliothek, Wolfenbuttel, has a number of bookplates as part of the Lessing Collection.[25] The Royal College of Physicians holds a collection of 2,000.

If the broadsheet was the simplest form for printed communication, then the leaflet and pamphlet may be regarded as the intermediary stages between it and a full-scale book. There is a plethora of examples of the use of this format and no lack of evidence of their being added to libraries. We have already noted the absence of this format in the medieval manuscript library, an indication of the lack of a large reading population to which this format was often directed. The Renaissance and moveable print changed all that. A very common use for tracts was to disseminate propaganda during political, religious, and social controversies, usually, though not exclusively, on the part of an opposition group.

The well-known collection of Thomason tracts in the British Museum, donated in 1762 by George III, totals some 30,000 books, pamphlets, and

newssheets. The items had been collected by a London bookseller, George
Thomason, during the years 1640-1661, a troubled period in English political history. The pains to which Thomason went in collecting the items
pay tribute to the private collector. On the one hand, he has been described
as "utterly indiscriminating"; on the other, Thomas Carlyle, who made extensive use of the collection in writing *Oliver Cromwell*, said, "I believe the
whole secret of the 17th Century is involved in that hideous mass of rub-
bish there."[26]

The Museum also has a similar collection of some 48,000 items, mainly
tracts and periodicals, covering the times of the French Revolution. The
collection is in three parts, the first acquired from a French collector in
1817 and the other two from John Wilson Croker in 1831 and 1856.[27]

The difficulties the institutional library has in administratively handling such collections is shown in a recent report of the National Library
of Scotland in which it is reported that "it has at last been possible to
undertake work on collections that were still uncatalogued . . . although
they had been in the library a long time." One collection to which this
statement refers is the Count Georg Septemus Dieterichs Collection of
books, tracts, academic dissertations, speeches, and announcements, printed
mainly in Germany and purchased by the Faculty of Advocates in 1819.
Reference is also made to the fact that cataloguing of seventeenth-century
pamphlets (4,000) had been completed and work on the eighteenth-cen-
tury material had begun.[28]

A sampling of Glasgow libraries provides further examples of pamphlet
collection. The Mitchell Library is credited with several large collections
relating to different religious controversies, a large number on political and
social questions, and, bought at auction from the library of a professor of
church history, 350 pamphlets on various subjects and eighty-nine on papal
aggression between 1847 and 1855. Stirling's Library has "several thousands" on British history and Scottish ecclesiastical matters; the library of
Mr. McGrigor has some 800 bound in sixty-nine volumes, two of which relate to the Holy Sepulchre and two to the Sabbath question; Mr. Shield's
library has five pamphlets on the case of Captain Green, executed for al-
leged piracy, a number of tracts on Porteous riots in 1736, a poetical
pamphlet on the execution of Thomas Aitkenhead for atheism in 1696,
and several more pamphlets on the Madeline Smith case.[29]

A modern version of the pamphlet is the report, a publication which
has very restricted distribution and which may often be duplicated rather

than printed. Duplication in microfilm is often valid. The outstanding collection in the United Kingdom is at the British Library, Lending Division, where there are 1 million (400,000 on microfiche).[30] This form of publication is mainly a product of science and technology and the main collections are in libraries devoted to those areas of knowledge. The Aeronautical Research Council holds 100,000; the Heating and Ventilating Research Association, 10,000.

If the pamphlet and leaflet were publications created to meet a growing demand from a more literate public, so too were the newspaper and periodical, publications designed to capture readers for continuous reading. The spectacular growth of these types of publication has been referred to in Chapter 4. It has been observed that "these periodicals were the industrial system, 'in book form,' with its division of labour and its sustained maximum output of articles manufactured from raw materials mechanically."[31]

The beginning of newspapers was in broadsheet or pamphlet form. The early seventeenth-century *Coranto,* a newssheet, was generally devoted to foreign news. Newspapers first appeared in Holland and Germany and by 1620 were appearing in England. At first they were printed half-sheet in folio, but later this became a quarto format.[32] The seventeenth century also saw the beginning of the periodical. From 1646 onward, printers were issuing catalogues of new books, often with commentaries added. The year 1665 saw the start of the regular publication of the *Journal des Scavans* in France, and *Acta Philosophica* and the Royal Society's *Philosophical Transactions* in Great Britain. The purpose of the last was "to give some account of the present undertakings, studies and labours of the Ingenious in many considerable parts of the world." The learned nature of these early issues is obvious. The eighteenth century saw the famous literary periodicals, the *Tatler* (1709), *Spectator* (1711), *Guardian* (1712) and *Examiner* (1710). These trends continued in the nineteenth century with the *Edinburgh Review* (1802) and *Blackwood's* (1817). The twentieth century saw the real explosion. [33] Not only has there been a tremendous increase in scientific and technical periodicals, but the demise of the literary periodical has been amply compensated for (in quantitive terms) by an exponential rise of the popular press. Children are now catered to by an ever-increasing number of comic books; the housewife is bombarded with housekeeping magazines and her husband with do-it-yourself magazines; and for all, infinite and instant gratification is provided by cheap pulp literature. For the dissemination of the pop arts (as the twentieth century refers to this area of literature), the periodical has taken over from the broadsheet, leaflet, and pamphlet of earlier times.

The importance of the serial form of publication to the library store is amply illustrated from statistics of the British Library, Reference Division. The Department of Printed Books has some 7 million volumes, of which there are 2 million monograph titles.[34] Even allowing for some duplication of monographs, over half of the volumes are therefore of serials. The space-consuming nature of such collections forced the library to its first "out-housing" venture: in 1905 it sent its holdings of newspapers published after 1800 to Colindale, where some 500,000 are housed. Most of this stock has been obtained by the legal deposit privilege, but some early issues have had to be otherwise acquired. Currently, the Reference Division acquires 25,000 periodical titles, a similar number being taken by the Lending Division.

As might be expected, in looking at our sample of Glasgow libraries, it is the two public libraries, Stirling's and the Mitchell, which have the fuller collections of periodicals, the private collectors mainly concentrating on those with a local interest.[35] As an example of how it is possible to specialize in collecting in this field, there is a small collection of some 400 newspapers published from the Western Front and prisoner-of-war camps (World War I) in La Bibliothèque et Musée de la Guerre.[36]

From the above classification of print-graphics, it can be seen how one group modulates into another—the broadside into the leaflet, the leaflet into the pamphlet, the pamphlet into the newspaper and periodical, and these into bound volumes, or codices. This is a well-known feature of classification systems. One further feature, which can be well illustrated by the concluding part of this chapter, is that very often, no matter which basic system is adopted, there remains a group of material which it is difficult to force into the classes created. Despite the very considerable coverage of the above forms, there still remain other items which find their way into the library store. These are often referred to as "printed ephemera," thus indicating that they are not to be considered worthwhile in the long term and, it therefore follows, not worthwhile to store in libraries. Yet it is to such material that the private collector has often turned with apparently fanatical enthusiasm, and often the institutional library has been later glad to acquire the collection. What were ephemera yesterday are the evidential data of today.

There is one really outstanding example of this in the United Kingdom—the John Johnson Collection of Printed Ephemera. In 1968 this
collection was transferred from the Oxford University Press to the Bodleian Library, which, suffering from overcrowding, had liquidated value-
less items only thirty years previously. The elimination process, ordered
by the curators, robbed the Bodleian of much of its ephemera, but due
to the conscience of a senior member of the staff, Strickland Gibson,
much of the discarded material was given to Johnson. Thirty years later,
the Bodleian was so pleased to have it back that it mounted an exhibition of the items in 1971.[37] Johnson was a true Oxford product; schooled
there, he won a scholarship to Exeter College and was graduated in 1904.
He had two brief years in the civil service in Egypt before returning to
Oxford with a senior demy scholarship at Magdalene College, part of his
duties being to take part in Egyptian archaeological excavations. It was
this work which impressed on him the importance of "trivial" evidence
and thus sowed the seeds for his collecting days. In 1914 he became an
assistant secretary to the University Press, and it was there that his interest in collecting was sharpened. By the 1930s he was fully committed to
hoarding "everything which would ordinarily go into the wastepaper bas-
ket after use, everything printed which is not actually a book. Another
way of describing it is to say that we gather everything which a museum
or a library would not ordinarily accept if it were offered as a gift."[38]
To Johnson's own collection others were added, and although he retired
in 1946, he worked on it until his death in 1956.

The items in the collection are truly remarkable. The surprise of a conventional librarian is effectively expressed in the following: "The Bodleian
library a few years ago was enriched with a collection of unique rarity
(in the true sense of this overworked word): the John Johnson collection
of printed ephemera."[39]

The organizer of the exhibition pointed out that the items exhibited
were merely representative of the whole collection.[40] If that was the case,
the following selective examples from the catalogue are merely indicative of the worth of the collection in terms of nonbook items:

(a) Heron-Allen Collection of Watch Papers
(b) E. Maude Hayter Collection of Valentine Cards
(c) M. L. Horn Collection of Cigarette Cards
(d) Sir John Evans Collection of Bank-Notes and Paper Money

(e) Ephemera, including special commemorative wrappings of the Great Exhibition, 1851

(f) A collection of copies of Paper Watermarks produced by carbon-14 process

(g) Booksellers' and Stationers' Trade Cards

(h) *The Weekly Account* No. 6, 11 October 1643 (one of the first newsbooks)

(i) A variety of Tax Labels & Stamps

(j) Holy pictures

(k) Hornbooks and Battledores

(l) Cheque Books

(m) Share Certificates

(n) Seed Catalogues

(o) Advertising Cards

(p) Cosmetic Labels

(q) Household Bills

(r) Tickets for Turnpikes (representative of tickets for all purposes)

(s) Theatre Programs and Tickets

(t) Bookies' Tickets

(u) Tickets for funerals of important personages

(v) Indulgence of 1508 printed by Pynson

(w) Trade Broadsheets

(x) Posters (e.g., "Attack on the Deadwood Stage," Buffalo Bill Cody and Annie Oakley)

(y) Schoolboys' Pieces (i.e., decorative blanks for child to add sample of own handwriting)

(z) Map of Narnia (the original drawn by C. S. Lewis about 1950)

While the catalogue gives no indication of the numbers of items in parts of the collection, the catalogue states that, on transfer to the Bodleian, there were 2,500 folio boxes, many with hundreds of items.[41]

It is difficult to give other examples since scant reference is made to this type of material in the literature on libraries, but there are one or two further examples of collections:

Lady Charlotte Schreiber's collection of fans and fan leaves and a collection of playing cards to the British Museum in 1891 and

1895 respectively, and in 1818 Miss Sarah Bank's collection of
visiting tickets, chap-bills, political cartoons and other ephemera.[42]
The Maidment collection of maps, pictures, pamphlets, tracts, leaflets, *cuttings and scraps* relating to Perthshire and Stirlingshire
in a total of 11 volumes in Mr. Gray's library, Glasgow.[43]

However, lack of mention in the literature does not mean to say that
there are not at least a few examples in most libraries. Pay a visit to any
library and ask the librarian for examples. Such a visit to the public reference library in Glasgow, the Mitchell, produced the following.

Simpson, William (Crimea Simpson): The marriage and coronation of
Alexander III; with other material related to Russia. 1883. [This is
a loose-leaf scrapbook with clippings from the *Illustrated London
News* and some 200 drawings and sketches, many originals of
Simpson]
Wotherspoon, James: In the track of the *Comet* on the Clyde, the West
Coast and the Channel. [Acquired by the Mitchell in the 1930s, this
is a fascinating work of fifty-one oblong folio volumes containing a
miscellaneous collection of pictures, plans, clippings, and textual
annotations]
Cockburn, William: Collection of old hard tartans. [This is a collection
of tartan cloths suitably mounted in folios]

Finally, there is an unusual item which does not appear in the British Museum catalogue:

Alken, Henry, and Sala, George Augustus: The funeral procession of
Arthur, Duke of Wellington, Ackermann, 1853. Two guineas.
66 feet x 5 inches, mounted on linen and housed in a slip case.
[This is the official guide to the funeral of November 18, 1852.]

So, despite the predominance of the codex, other formats have found
a place in libraries, either because their knowledge content was considered important or because of a more or less well-defined objective of a collector. Exactly the same principle holds good for the production of new
media created by the photographic and electronic age.

NOTES

1. Scholderer, V., *Johann Gutenberg: The Inventor of Printing* (British Museum, 1963), Pl. VII and VIII.
2. Binns, N. E., *An Introduction to Historical Bibliography* (Association of Assistant Librarians, 1953), pp. 220-221.
3. Great Britain, Department of Education and Science, *The Scope for Automatic Data Processing in the British Library* (Her Majesty's Stationery Office, 1972), p. 625, Table 4.
4. Baumfield, B. H., and McColvin, K. R., *Library Students' London,* 2nd ed. (Association of Assistant Librarians, 1969), p. 89.
5. United States, Library of Congress, *Annual Report of the Librarian of Congress, 1969* (Library of Congress, 1970), p. 1.
6. Baumfield and McColvin, *Library Students' London* p. 88.
7. Francis, F., ed., *Treasures of the British Museum* (Thames and Hudson, 1971), p. 285.
8. Ibid., p. 293.
9. Ibid., p. 307.
10. Hind, A. M., *The Processes and Schools of Engraving* (British Museum, 1952), p. 15.
11. Burton, M., *Famous Libraries of the World* (Grafton, 1937), p. 442.
12. Baumfield, and McColvin, *Library Students' London,* p. 41.
13. Burton, *Famous Libraries of the World,* p. 11.
14. Ibid., p. 104.
15. These examples have been taken from Mason, T., *Public and Private Libraries of Glasgow* (T. D. Morison, 1885), pp. 291, 380-381, 243, 229.
16. Burton, *Famous Libraries of the World,* p. 409.
17. Hobbs, J. L., *Local History and the Library* (Deutsch, 1962), p. 41.
18. Hobson, A., *Great Libraries* (Weidenfeld and Nicholson, 1970), p. 64.
19. Burton, *Famous Libraries of the World,* p. 104.
20. Ibid., p. 409.
21. Ibid., p. 51.
22. Ibid., p. 143.
23. Mason, *Public and Private Libraries of Glasgow,* p. 229.
24. Ibid., p. 282.
25. Francis, *Treasures of the British Museum,* pp. 215, 233.
26. Rawlings, G. B., *The British Museum Library* (Grafton, 1916), pp. 111-117.
27. Ibid., pp. 124-130.
28. National Library of Scotland, *Annual Report 1970-71,* p. 8.
29. Mason, *Public and Private Libraries of Glasgow,* pp. 95, 322, and passim.
30. Great Britain, Department of Education and Science, *The Scope for Automatic Data Processing,* p. 625, Table 4.
31. Toynbee, A., *A Study of History,* rev. ed. (Book Club Associates, 1972), p. 30.
32. Landau, T., *Encyclopedia of Librarianship,* 2nd rev. ed. (Bowes, 1961), p. 104.

33. *Encyclopaedia Britannica* (1947) vol. 17., "Periodical," pp. 512-516.
34. Great Britain, Department of Education and Science, *The Scope for Automatic Data Processing,* p. 625, Table 4.
35. Mason, *Public and Private Libraries of Glasgow,* passim.
36. Burton, *Famous Libraries of the World,* p. 395.
37. Bodleian Library, *The John Johnson Collection: Catalogue of an Exhibition* (Bodleian Library, 1971).
38. Ibid., p. 11.
39. Roberts, R. J., "Recent Work in Rare Book Librarianship" in *Library Association Record* (February 1973), p. 25.
40. Bodleian Library, *The John Johnson Collection,* p. 4.
41. Ibid.
42. Francis, *Treasures of the British Museum,* p. 293.
43. Mason, *Public and Private Libraries of Glasgow,* p. 288.

10
The Photographic and Electronic Era

The invention and development of photography in the nineteenth century had far-reaching effects on the world of graphic illustration. So far as the fine arts were concerned, it introduced an element of realism and exactitude in copying which made the artist somewhat superfluous and turned him to a more and more surrealistic style. McLuhan vividly described photography as a "brothel-without-walls." The effect on the production of prints was also considerable. Whether the illustration was for book, pamphlet, broadsheet, or periodical, it was now no longer necessary to have someone cut a wood block, engrave or etch a metal plate, or draw on a stone; the artist in this sense was now redundant, and almost anyone with a camera could produce photographic prints which in turn could be transferred photographically to a printing plate, which could then be prepared for either relief, intaglio, or planographic printing. The increase in illustrations in books, particularly in popular periodicals and newspapers, was very considerable.

Libraries also became collectors of illustrated books, and in many instances they have collected separate prints as fine art or as historical data. The photographic print was merely a technological extension of the ink print, and it was inevitable that it too should be collected; examples are relatively easy to find. Before citing a cross section of these, it should be pointed out that the illustration collection in a modern library may well be a mixture of photographic prints, ink prints, and illustrations cannibalized from books, periodicals, and newspapers. It may also include negative transparency masters from which photographic prints are produced. It is possible that it also includes the positive transparency, or lantern slide, which is used for enlarged projection onto a screen.

It is the present-day library which offers examples of the graphics pro-

duced by the photographic and electronic techniques, and London and
South-East England provide almost perfect sample areas, offering an excellent cross section of all types of libraries.

Fortunately, there exist some good directories of libraries in these areas
and, more fortunately, one of them, published by the Library Association,
specifically lists materials other than books and periodicals.[1] Extensive
use has been made of this work, so much so that if no reference is made
for a given example, it can be assumed to have come from it.

It appears that the largest single collection of photographs in the United
Kingdom is that of the Imperial War Museum, Photographic Library. A
total of some 3 million items is something of a monument to dedicated
collecting with a relatively narrow objective for a noncommercial purpose.
The fact that it is limited to coverage of the two world wars and other
British and Commonwealth wars from 1914 makes it all the more remarkable that it is such a large collection and gives some indication of what
might be available in other subjects. The size is all the more exceptional
when compared with the 3,070,000 photographic prints, negatives, and
slides of the U.S. Library of Congress.[2] The Ministry of Public Buildings
and Works has a collection of 500,000 items in its photographic library,
all relating to buildings designed by, and ancient monuments in care of,
the Ministry. The Central Office of Information has a collection of 300,000
black-and-white photographs, mainly on social and economic conditions
in Britain and the Commonwealth; the Commonwealth Office has 27,000
prints and 2,300 negatives.

As would be expected, there are some large collections in libraries which
specialize in the fine arts. The Courtauld Insititute of Art has 900,000 re-
productions of paintings and drawings (The Witt collection), 473,000 re-
productions of architecture, sculpture, and illuminated manuscripts (The
Conway Library), and some 22,000 photographs in a teaching collection. The
Victoria and Albert Museum has 300,000 photographs; the Warburg Institute, 200,000.

Two further subjects in which there are large collections are geography
and natural history. The Royal Geographical Society has a collection of
100,000; the British Museum of Natural History has 250,000.

It was not only the more obvious subjects which attracted illustrations.
The Aluminium Federation has many photographs, and the Bee Research
Association has some 5,000 pictures.

The interest of the popular press in illustrations is shown by the *Daily*

Mirror's collection of 804,000 photographs and 600,000 negatives. The new medium of television also needs stills, and the BBC reference library has a collection of 300,000, most of which were acquired by the purchase of the library of the Hulton *Picture Post* when it ceased publication as a popular news-picture magazine. ATV Network Limited, one of the program companies producing for the Independent Broadcasting Authority, has a small collection of 14,000.

Many public libraries have collections of illustrations, either of a general nature, mainly for use by children and schoolteachers, or attached to the local history collection, where an attempt at comprehensiveness has forced their inclusion. The largest is at Birmingham where 300,000 illustrations form part of a visual-aids department.[3] It is mainly used by schoolteachers, who may borrow up to 100 at a time.

Aerial photography is a specialized form. La Bibliothèque et Musée de la Guerre in Paris holds aerial photographs as part of its map collection (aerial photographs are often used as a basis for map production); there are 10,500 items.[4] The British Ministry of Housing and Local Government has a special library devoted to aerial photographs.

Negative transparencies are a means to an end in that they act as an intermediary master for the production of prints. Positive transparencies, on the other hand, are intended to be the end product. The image almost always must be enlarged by projection through a lens. Such an enlargement can be considerable, and so positive transparencies are particularly useful for showing to groups of people, often as an adjunct to a lecture. Desk-model enlargers are available for individual use. Unfortunately, as often happens in technological progress, there has been no standardization of size of transparencies and the variations create problems. Originally called lantern slides, positive transparencies are commonly referred to nowadays simply as slides and come in three mount sizes, 3¼" x 3¼", 2¾" x 2¾", and 2" x 2". It is possible to have different sizes of transparency in each of these mounts. As a part of the illustrations collection at Birmingham, there are 54,000 of the older 3¼" x 3¼" size and a number of the now much more common 2" x 2". Subject areas which were well endowed with prints also have slides. The Royal Geographical Society has a collection of 50,000 (3¼" x 3¼") together with some 30,000 negatives. The Architectural Association has 40,000, and, of course, the fine arts collections provide a number of examples, the largest being at Senate House, London University, which has an extensive collection of 176,000.[5]

The filmstrip is a length of 35mm. film on which a series of photographs

is framed and processed to a positive image for projection. The strips of
film can be relatively easily duplicated and therefore this format is very
useful for publishing multiple copies of strips with photographs pertaining to a particular topic. Printed notes are often available to complement
the illustrations.

Filmstrips are most often used in education, particularly, though not exclusively, at the elementary and secondary levels. Many schools have their
own collections, but some education authorities have organized central
or regional libraries of strips. A number of public libraries maintain collections. A survey conducted by the Library Association in 1971 found
that 43 of 389 public library systems held filmstrips. Twenty-eight loaned
to schools as well as others, eighteen only to schools.[6] The largest collection, around 4,000, was in a county library. Another survey of college
libraries found that out of 607, over 30 percent had filmstrips.[7] No other
type of audiovisual material was so widely represented.

Technologically, the filmstrip is a by-product of the movie industry and
so the 35mm. film is standard. Thus, the production of large quantities has
reduced the price to a level where it has become a very attractive proposition for the still photographer. Reduction in the size of equipment and
the cheapness of materials allow anyone who wishes to become a photographer.

The movie film is of much more sociological significance than the still,
yet it is of less importance to libraries. Still photography certainly allowed
a tremendous increase in the number of visual graphics, but only the slide
was for group viewing. The movie was really for the masses. In the movie,
two new dimensions were added, movement and, later, speech. As a medium of communication, it was much easier to receive than the printed word
and more stimulating than the still. Up until its invention, only newspapers
and magazines were aimed at mass markets. The movie was the first serious challenger produced by the new technology. As with any medium,
it can be used to communicate the serious, the less serious, and the trivial;
it can be used to inform or to gratify. The movie was used for all of these,
but most movies were produced by the Hollywood "dream factory," and
the financial success which ensued saw to it that other countries followed
with similar productions. Until the advent of television, cinema audiences
remained very large. In the United Kingdom in 1945, the number of cinema admissions was 1,585 million for the year, an average of thirty times
a year, nearly once a week, for every man, woman, and child. This was,

of course, at the end of World War II, when all entertainment was experiencing a boom, and just before the introduction of television broadcasting, which has been the major factor in reducing movie audiences (273 million in 1967).[8]

The products of the dream factories were seldom stored in libraries, however, except for the stores of the producing companies. In many instances, it would be considered that the gratification level would be too low, but there was also a technological difficulty. The 35mm. film necessitated large, sophisticated, and expensive projection equipment which made its use difficult. The smaller formats of 16mm. and 8mm., which were later introduced, relieved this problem to some extent, and it is more often these formats which are found in libraries unless the store is for archival purposes. The U.S. Library of Congress has 97,000 reels of motion pictures, and the British Museum apparently none or very few, since they are not mentioned in published statistics of stocks.[9] In the United Kingdom, one of the largest collections is at the British Film Institute where, in the National Film Archive, there are 8,000 title films and 10,000 newsreels in addition to a loan collection of 1,600 titles in 35mm. and 16mm. There is also a collection of 600,000 stills at the Institute. A survey of college libraries in the United Kingdom revealed that 6.8 percent of the 607 libraries surveyed stocked movies, while a survey of public libraries showed that some 50 of 389 stocked movies, mostly 16mm., but some 8mm.[10] The largest collection in the public libraries was 300. Compared with other graphics, movies are not a large part of the library store.

Another by-product of the 35mm. film produced by the movie industry was the miniaturization of records. The microfilm was the first of a number of different kinds of microforms. The process offered a number of advantages to libraries (see Chapter 4, pp. 46-47). Later developments in format were the microcard, a sheet opaque with a photo-image; the microprint, a sheet opaque with an ink image; and the microfiche, a sheet transparency. Although their major use was to miniaturize existing records, occasionally they were employed for first publication. Considerable readers' resistance to the use of the hardware has been encountered, but other advantages (not least of which is the fact that a miniaturized record is sometimes all that is available) have seen to it that libraries have stocked them.

In 1969 the U.S. Library of Congress held 418,000 sheets (fiche and

opaques), and also 330,000 films and strips.[11] The British Museum registers its holdings at 2,500 shelf feet, the National Reference Library of
Science and Invention at 300,000 fiche, 100 films, and 80,000 microcards,
and the National Lending Library of Science and Technology holds 160
miles, or the equivalent of 100,000 volumes.[12] The different methods of
presenting these statistics make comparisons difficult, but they do show
that national libraries are affected by these new media. Perhaps this difficulty helps to explain why a good number of universities do not specify
their microform holdings in directories.

Despite the fact that the original is in stock, a library may well have a
miniaturized copy so that the original may be protected from unnecessary
use. Dr. Williams' Library, and Eton College, Windsor, both have micro-
records of some of their manuscript material. Research libraries often
have files, as at the Glasshouse Crops Research Institute where microfilms
of relevant American M.Sc. and Ph.D. theses are kept. Public libraries often
have at least their own local newspapers on microfilm and, quite frequently,
a microfilm of a complete run of the London *Times*.

There are two isolated, minor, but pertinent examples of the use of
miniaturized records: the National Library of Scotland reports that it has
a microfilm record of the scrapbooks, 1943-1951, of the Citizen's Theatre,
Glasgow; and Cambridge University Library holds microfilm copies of the
BBC reports by its monitoring service, 1939-1952.[13] Regarding the latter,
it is claimed that they "will make available to research workers a complete file of an incomparable source for all who are interested in contemporary history."[14]

The microfilming of the London *Times* is an example of publishing
in this medium. But for this venture, many libraries would otherwise have
had to do without files of this supreme example of the fourth estate. The
concept of this kind of miniaturized package has been repeated in a number of other ventures. The Readex Microprint Corporation of America
offers for sale a more or less complete set of British Parliamentary Papers
of the eighteenth and nineteenth centuries and is in the process of preparing a set for the years from 1901 to 1922.[15] The format used is sheet
opaque and the image is an ink print. Another of its publications is
Early American Imprints, a microprint package of all American books,
pamphlets, and broadsheets from the introduction of printing in the
United States in 1639 up to 1900.

A recent venture in the United Kingdom has been undertaken by the

Harvester Primary Social Sources. Their first package of 260 microfiches is entitled *Britain in Europe Since 1945* and holds in miniature some 22,000 pages of primary source material issued by sixty-nine British pressure groups. Future packages promised are *Alternative/Underground Press, Poverty,* and *Peace and Liberation Movements.*[16] Such packages are an attractive method of purchase for any library likely to have research workers, and many will be bought. An evaluation of the usefulness of "packaged libraries" in microform is being undertaken in a Washington library which has received a $40,000 grant to investigate the package *The Library of American Civilization.* This package is published by Library Resources Incorporated, a subsidiary of Encyclopaedia Britannica. It is produced on ultramicrofiche by the PCMI process and successfully packages 20,000 volumes (6 million pages).[17] It offers a desktop library which should be a boon to any research worker in the subject. More series are planned.

As the invention of photography increased the scope for the visual presentation of material, so did electromagnetic techniques break new ground in recording sound. In truth, this was a real breakthrough in that up until the invention of the gramophone, it was not possible for libraries to store audio signals. It was 1821 when Michael Faraday began his experiments with electromagnetism, which led to the electric telegraphs of Cooke and Wheatstone in 1837, the invention of the telephone by Alexander Bell in 1876, and the invention of the phonograph by Thomas Edison in 1877. The phonograph was an instrument to play back audio signals which had been recorded on a spiral groove continuously circling a brass drum. The brass drum was succeeded by a wax cylinder, and then in 1887 Emile Berliner produced the disc, or gramophone record, which by 1897 was a commercial success, as it still is to the present day, although it is now being challenged by magnetic tape as a recording medium.

Any drums or cylinders which now exist in libraries are museum pieces. The signals on them were probably rerecorded on discs; indeed early disc recordings were often rerecorded on new discs as technical improvements were made. This is particularly the case with old 78 r.p.m. discs, which have been rerecorded on the long-play 33 1/3 r.p.m. discs or have been transferred to tape.

The largest bulk of recordings is of music rather than the spoken voice, an indication perhaps of society's search for gratification. It is natural, therefore, that in the early days of recording, libraries eschewed the new medium, apart from a few that had a special interest and some which stored a few records of archival significance.

The library with the largest collection is that of the BBC. Sociologically, the adaptation of electromagnetism to broadcasting is more significant than its use for recording. By 1895 Marconi had established wireless communication, by 1898 signals were transmitted across the English Channel, and by 1901 across the Atlantic. By 1922, the technology was so advanced that it was possible to broadcast to the mass population, and the BBC was formed in that year. Later, in 1926, it was reestablished as a public corporation. Because it was using audio signals, it was natural to record its broadcasts for possible future use and also to use material recorded by other producers and publishers. This led to the establishment of libraries specifically to store audiographics. The BBC Gramophone Record Library now has a stock of 800,000 discs and is adding to the store at the rate of 30,000 per month.[18] It buys every recording published in the United Kingdom. In the Sound Archives Library there are also 30,000 recordings of "historical" sounds recorded by the BBC itself.

Some other examples of specialized stocks are City of London College, 40 language records; HM Customs and Excise, Linguaphone records for French and German; Senate House, London University, 5,500 records; British Council Music Library, 900 discs for loan; British Institute of Recorded Sound, 180,000 recordings.

The escalation of growth of gramophone record libraries took place after 1948, the year of the introduction of the long-play records which made it a much more feasible proposition for public libraries to have loan collections. By 1968 some 165 authorities (out of a possible 400) were operating such libraries with a total stock of over 700,000 discs (an average of over 4,500 each).[19] As usual, it was the London public libraries which tended to pioneer innovations, and some of the largest stocks are there. Westminster Public Library has some 25,000 and Camden 29,000.

As a final example of how some libraries have eschewed this new medium, one only needs to compare the U.S. Library of Congress with the British Library. The Library of Congress holds 2,001,000 talking books, 267,000 recordings on discs, tapes, and wires, and 14,000 books on tape, the British Library—none.[20]

The Library of Congress groups discs, tapes, and wires together, since all are audio recordings. It may be that in some of the other statistics quoted above, tapes have been included, but they are in much less evidence in library stocks. A survey of record libraries shows that only eleven held tapes, and only one of these tapes, in cassette form.[21] A survey of college libraries found that about 11 percent of the 607 surveyed had audio tapes (the majority almost certainly for language instruction).[22] There are further examples from the London area: English Folk Dance and Song Society, 72 tapes; Civic Trust, 17 tapes of archival nature; and British Institute of Recorded Sound, a collection of tapes. The likelihood is that many more libraries have small collections which they consider too insignificant to mention in directories.

It was noted above that only one public library in 1968 held cassette tapes. By 1971 the number had risen to five, and speculation is that it is likely to be a more manageable medium for libraries than the disc.[23] The sound quality from the cassette tape is, at the moment, not so good as that of the disc, but there has been a good improvement over the last few years. Given the same rate of progress, it will not be long before it is of equal quality.

Exciting and significant as the breakthrough and developments in sound broadcasting and recording have been, they have been surpassed by similar developments in the visual communications field. To James Logie Baird goes much of the credit for pioneer work in television broadcasting. The first demonstration was in 1926 and by 1928 transatlantic transmission had taken place. The first public broadcast was in 1936 by the BBC, but it was not till the postwar era that television was fully operational as a mass medium. As with sound broadcasting, visual broadcasting is capable of being recorded, and it is axiomatic that all broadcasting companies will have kept copies of their own programs. Unlike sound recordings, however, there are very few other producers of visual recordings. The difficulties have been in the development of a suitable playback deck at a reasonable cost and technical problems in the standardization of the recording media.

A public library survey found only one library holding video recordings.[24]

It is perhaps appropriate here to point out that, generally, the United States is more advanced than the United Kingdom in the application of new techniques. This fact is exemplified by the previous comparisons of their respective national libraries.

NOTES

1. Library Association, Reference, Special and Information Section, South Eastern Group, *Library Resources in London and the South East* (Library Association, 1969), passim.

2. United States, Library of Congress, *Annual Report of Librarian of Congress, 1969* (Library of Congress, 1970), p. 1.
3. Birmingham Public Libraries, *Service to Teachers* (n. d.) (leaflet).
4. Burton, M., *Famous Libraries of the World* (Grafton, 1937), p. 143.
5. *ASLIB Directory,* 3rd ed. (Aslib, 1970), p. 243.
6. Hutchinson, A. "Audio-visual Materials in Public Libraries in the U.K.," in *Library and Information Bulletin,* No. 13 (Library Association, 1971), p. 2.
7. "Survey of College Libraries in the U.K., 1970," in *Library and Information Bulletin* No. 15 (Library Association, 1971), p. 11.
8. Jarvie, I. C., *Towards a Sociology of the Cinema* (Routledge, 1970), p. 116.
9. United States, Library of Congress, *Annual Report 1969* (Library of Congress, 1970), p. 1.
10. "Survey of College Libraries in the U.K., 1970," p. 11, and Hutchinson, *Audio-visual Materials,* p. 3.
11. United States, Library of Congress, *Annual Report 1969,* p. 1.
12. Great Britain, Department of Education and Science, *The Scope for Automatic Data Processing in the British Library* (Her Majesty's Stationery Office, 1972), p. 625.
13. National Library of Scotland, *Annual Report, 1970-71,* p. 56, Cambridge University, *Library Information Bulletin No. 18* (August 1973), p. 13.
14. Cambridge University, *Library Information Bulletin No. 18,* p. 13.
15. Ollé J. G., *Introduction to British Government Publications,* 2nd ed. (Association of Assistant Librarians, 1973), pp. 135-136.
16. Harvester Primary Social Sources, *Progress Report 1* (leaflet).
17. *National Council for Reprography and Documentation (NCRd) Bulletin* (Spring 1972), p. 31.
18. Curral, H. F. J., and King, A. H., *Gramophone Record Libraries,* 2nd ed. (Crosby Lockwood, 1970), p. 226.
19. "Gramophone Record Libraries in the U.K.," in *Library and Information Bulletin No. 11* (Library Association, 1970), p. 10.
20. United States, Library of Congress, *Annual Report 1969,* p. 1.
21. "Gramophone Record Libraries in the U.K.," p. 10.
22. "Survey of College Libraries in the U.K., 1970," p. 11.
23. Hutchinson, *Audio-visual Materials,* p. 2.
24. Ibid., p. 3.

Part Four

FEEDBACK FROM THE MEMORY

11

Access to the Stock

The concept of feedback is readily identified in general systems theory.[1] Feedback occurs when the output or behavior of a system is returned to the system as input which in turn affects succeeding output. Feedback mainly occurs in open systems, that is, those which are in communication with their environment, taking input from it and giving output to it. This mainly happens in living systems, which take the necessary life-supporting substances from the environment, process them through the system, extracting what it needs, and then excreting back to the environment that which it does not want—in other words, a life cycle. The concept also applies to the nonliving physical world. An atom can exist without throughput, but throughputs do occur in that electrons can be passed from atom to atom to give electric current. The atom is merely acting as an agency for a force, whereas in a life system the throughput acts to sustain the force.

Applying the concept to libraries as systems, it is clear that they are more analogous to life systems. The reason for this is that they are models of part of a life system. This is apparent from the previous analysis of the three communication systems in Chapter 2. It was noted there that the library store was created by man as a substitute for his own memory. Chapter 3 sketched the remarkable story of the development of communications, noting that, as man's brain developed, his knowledge increased but his memory proved poor for the vast amounts of data he was collecting. He therefore modeled his libraries to be part of his memory and thus they work, by general analogy, in the same way. There is an input, throughput, and output, and the output of knowledge recycles further thought and the re-creation of knowledge which, when recorded, is fed back into the library system.

General systems theory has analyzed some specific kinds of feedback, one of which has already been dealt with.[2] Amplification of a system is defined as the use of a local source in feeding back input. In terms of libraries, this is the cooperative use of the resources of other libraries.

Also identified are the concepts of negative and positive feedback. Negative feedback applies when a secondary input counteracts the main system, as would happen with the braking system in a machine. Positive feedback supplements and helps a main system. An example of this would be the "running start" sometimes given to a motor car when the ignition system has failed because of loss of battery power. This is a difficult concept to relate to libraries. Quantitative growth is positive feedback, but in terms of improving the quality of the memory, there must be elements of negative feedback because new knowledge received may in fact be incorrect or made more obscure. Increased size has also created additional problems of retrieval, and there could be an argument that this has decreased the quality of a memory. The positive nature of the growth must clearly outweigh these negative examples, and so a library memory has, in the main, a positive feedback.

Feedback systems can also be seen as goal-seeking or goal-changing. A thermostat in a heating system feeds back information about the temperature reached by the output so that the goal of a constant temperature can be maintained. Goal-changing occurs when a system modifies itself in order to aim at a different objective, the best example being the evolution of life forms in adapting themselves to suit their ever-changing environment. As man is both goal-seeking and goal-changing, so is his library system. In searching his memory, he will have some predetermined objective for the data he wishes to retrieve, and in many instances the use of this data will make him change goals. The chapters on the effect of the library system will deal more fully with the latter point.

Feedback is therefore an essential part of the library system, and this facet of the system must be very carefully controlled if the system is to have its full value. An understanding of how a library feeds back to its readers reveals many of the problems of the management of libraries and is therefore the essence of the work of the librarian. The methods and techniques he uses in the organization of his library should always be designed so that a maximum feedback is achieved.

There must be the fullest and easiest access to the memory if the system is to work to its maximum value. In other words, maximum retrieval is necessary.

If the ultimate theoretical aim of the profession of librarianship is to ensure that every single member of society has access to the library memory, then this has been achieved to some extent in the developed countries of the world. Chapter 4 on the growth of libraries traced the various stages until the nineteenth-century emergence of a public tax-supported system of libraries with access to all as one of its prime purposes. By cooperative techniques with other libraries, they can give access to the total store of a nation and, if necessary, of foreign libraries. This is an excellent situation; however, as with most ideals, when other detailed aspects of access to the store are examined, there are many practical problems.

Before looking at some of these problems, it should be reiterated that the nearest approach to the ideal obtains only in developed countries. Chapter 4 gave some statistics of the underdeveloped nature of some countries in terms of illiteracy and lack of libraries. History would suggest that they will develop toward the ideal state. There are further examples of how a society can fall short of the ideal even though it may be considered developed. This occurs when a section of the population is denied access, or its access is limited, to library provision.

It is natural that libraries which limit their function to serve only a section of society should limit total access. This happens in academic libraries. special libraries, and even in some national libraries. The latter should, by definition, give access to all, but by reason of geographical situation and also limitations of size of the building, some restrictions on free access have to be made. The British Library, Reference Division, is open only to persons over the age of twenty-one and to those who have acquired a pass. Passes are issued only to people who have given some evidence that the particular kind of research they wish to undertake can be done only there and not in some other library which may be readily accessible. This kind of limitation on access is of practical necessity and is not a ban on access to the total library store, since potential readers who may be refused a pass will be directed elsewhere.

Academic libraries have a long tradition of allowing access to bona fide readers, although the tradition is one which grew with the increase in the number of books and the increase in literacy, which, coupled together, created demand. In the beginning it was different. In the fifteenth cen-

tury, Oxford gave study facilities to "only graduates and people in religious orders who have studied philosophy for eight years."[3] Nowadays,
not only is the bona fide reader welcomed, but any member of the public may have a right of access, not only morally because the greater part
of the income of academic institutions comes from public funds, but also,
in the United Kingdom, legally, since the library receives a 10 percent
discount on its book purchases in return for allowing public access. In
some cases only reference use is allowed.

   Despite the theory that there should be complete access to public tax-
supported library systems, two qualifications should be noted. In some
countries, because of social and political discrimination, some portion of
the population may be denied or have restricted access to public libraries.
Examples of this situation can be found in the United States and in South
Africa. In 1963 the American Library Association found it necessary to
appoint a committee of inquiry "to examine the scope and extent of limited access to public libraries throughout the United States, with particular reference to the problem of racial segregation in Southern Libraries."[4]
A book on South African libraries finds it necessary to devote one of its
chapters to library service for nonwhites.[5]

   The second qualification is that the qualitative standards of stock of public
libraries is such that access is discouraged to a section of the community.
This is a criticism often leveled at the public libraries of the United
Kingdom. While there are a few historical examples of subscription sections within public libraries, the movement has always been toward free
use, an ideal which is staunchly adhered to by the profession, as witnessed
by its fight against public-lending right (i.e., the right of an author to receive
a monetary reward for the loans of his books by public libraries). Despite this, at any one time, only some 25 percent of the population is likely
to be in membership, and it is held that this is because the standard of
stock is aimed at middle-class reading standards. A survey of the public
libraries of the United Kingdom contains an analysis of members and nonmembers by intelligence groups.[6] Even making allowances for the crud-
ity of methods of categorizing people in this fashion, it is clear that membership comes mainly from the top echelons. Categorizing people into
ten intelligence groups, the survey found that the highest group had a membership rate of 62 percent, the bottom group a rate of 15 percent.[7] The
same survey found that 21 percent of its sample of nonmembers were critical of the public library because of the fact that the books they wanted

were not available. Interestingly, a higher percentage (40) of members made the same criticism.[8] A similar survey found that, of a sample of lapsed members, 16 percent gave "Could not get books" as a reason.[9] Neither survey takes the problem further by investigating what type of book is lacking, but it needs no stretch of imagination to guess that, in the main, it is that type of publication which is usually referred to as "subliterature." The following extract illustrates the point well. It is taken from Richard Hoggart's work, and he is writing of the "Juke-Box Boys."

> What are such men likely to read, apart from picture-dailies, the more sensational Sunday paper, and newspaper/magazine? The public library has no appeal, nor even perhaps the stationers' four-penny libraries whose main function is to hold a large stock of the kinds of fiction—"Crime" or "Tec" or "Mystery", "Westerns" and "Romance" or "Love" as the shelves are usually headed— of which public libraries never have enough copies. One needs to look rather at those "magazine shops" of which there is always one in every large working-class shopping-area . . . there is a rough division of material into three themes—Crime, Science Fiction, and Sex Novelettes.[10]

There is obviously considerable justification in the argument that the public library is middle-class, and it might be possible to attract more members if stocks were increased to contain the pulp or subculture literature which is read by a wide section of the population. Whether this is done depends on the prevailing view of what effect society wishes its public library system to have. It is enough at the moment to quote the view of one of the most important pioneers of the public library systems in the United Kingdom. During the proceedings of the Select Committee on Public Libraries of 1849, the following verbal exchange took place.

William Ewart
You stated in your last examination that English literary men had, in your opinion, suffered much from the limited number and inaccessibility of public libraries. Do you consider that the English people must have suffered greatly from the same cause?

Edward Edwards
I think, very much indeed: and I believe that the want of ac-
cessibility of good books is one cause of the backwardness of
this country in respect to education among large portions of the
population, and it is one reason why, in cases where some sort
of schooling has been obtained, it has been found, upon the
Parliamentary inquiries which have been made into the state of
education in certain districts of the country, that such schooling
has been of little use to the children in after life, nothing like a
taste for reading having been cultivated. I think access to good
libraries would be one great means of advancing the *educational*
condition of the country.[11]

The last sentence shows clearly what Edwards felt about the importance of access.
Now for some of the practicalities of achieving maximum access
to stock.
The physical situation of the library can have a limiting effect if a bad
site is chosen. This is particularly the case with public libraries. Many examples can be found of libraries which should be achieving the same numbers
of issues from the lending department, but where in fact there are large
differences caused by one building being placed on a site which is not so
close to the main flow of pedestrian and vehicular traffic as the other.
This reduces the number of readers who come to the library since there
are limits to the distance which people are prepared to travel. While the
effects of bad location are most clearly seen in the public library sector,
the principle equally applies to any other type of library. All writers on
the subject of library planning and design make it clear that the choice
of a good site is of paramount importance. The location of public libraries is now considered of such importance that it warrants a standard. The
International Federation of Library Associations recommends setting up
branch libraries in urban areas "for populations of 5,000 and in rural
areas for populations of 500 and over unable to readily use a larger library
with two miles."[12]
The recent controversy over the location of the new building for the
British Library, Reference Division, provides a good example. As a national library, it should be available to everyone in the United Kingdom and
there is, therefore a practical choice of only three sites. It should be

placed in some provincial city near the center of the country or, alternatively, it should be situated in the largest conurbation, London, with a
choice between central London or a suburb, the latter being the cheaper.
Having researched the uses of the British Library, Reference Division, the
Dainton Committee (set up by the British government to make recommendations on the future of national libraries) ascertained that 66 percent
of users were London University staff and research workers, with the
same percentage from the London postal area.[13] This led the committee
to recommend that the new National Reference Library be situated in
central London, where they believe the stocks would be most heavily used.

The number of hours a library opens its doors to its readership is a
factor in controlling access to the stock. One report on university libraries
admits to defeat in laying down absolute standards and recommends that
"each university library should meet its demand as far as is practically possible and should consider seriously whether libraries should not extend
their evening and week-end hours."[14] It found "a lack of standardisation
and lack of agreement," which is not surprising since the practical problem
must be solved by means of a cost/benefit analysis (i.e., the cost of keeping
the building open in relation to the number of readers using it).[15]

Different committees will view the ratio differently and the balance
will be decided by subjective judgment. One interesting compromise is
noted by the report. At Hull, one room, with study facilities but no books,
is kept open when the library is closed.[16] A somewhat similar situation
exists at the new Science Library of Aberdeen University. A suite of
individual study carrels is designed in such a way that they can be separated from the main library, apart from one room of reference books, so
that round-the-clock access is available to those who are provided with keys.

For public libraries, a recent report is much more specific. District libraries serving populations of 25,000+ should be open at least 60 hours
her week; branch libraries serving populations of over 4,000, 30 to 60
hours; branch libraries serving between 1,000 and 4,000, 10 to 30 hours;
and mobile libraries should stop for at least 15 minutes and visit each
stopping point at least once a fortnight.[17]

One important factor in considering opening hours is the balance of
reference and lending stock; those libraries which maintain large reference collections must attempt to extend opening hours, those which lend
freely may not be so concerned. Which method gives the better access
to stock is open to debate. A lending system, which allows a borrower

to remove stock from the library and thus gives him a 24-hour-a-day access, at the same time effectively denies access to borrowed books to all other readers. Almost all libraries compromise on this problem, lending some part of their stock and keeping others for reference only. In general terms, libraries which stock books for casual reading will operate loan services, and those operating study and research facilities will be for reference only. As examples, the mobile-library services of public libraries will be almost totally on a loan basis, perhaps only a few information works being kept for reference only; at the other end of the scale, a national reference library will be almost totally devoted to reference works.

The value of a reference collection to research workers is apparent from the 200 years of nonlending by the British Museum Library.

One might have expected the two other large university research libraries of the United Kingdom to be reference libraries. Not so—on the one hand, the Bodleian, at Oxford, is reference, on the other, Cambridge is lending. A report on university libraries seems to favor loan service. It recommended that vacation postal-loan services should be increased, particularly for students living at a distance from large towns.[18]

A further problem is the question of open or closed access. Obviously, the more open stock is, the greater value it has for readers, especially those who like to browse among the stock and use it in a casual fashion. Against this advantage one must weigh the disadvantage of the loss of stock. It appears that many of the early libraries, from that of Assurbanipal onward, were open-access. There were two reasons for this: the size of stock was not sufficiently large to merit consideration of more economical storage methods, and since access to the library was for the "elite" only, there was less chance of theft. Even the early public libraries could be used only by the literate elite.

There is some evidence that locking up books is an early practice. The standard work on book storage and protection pays scant attention in the text to this point, but an examination of the plates shows evidence of locks. An illustration of a Roman *capsa* (book-box) apparently shows a lock for fastening the lid. In three other plates, book presses apparently have locks (one from the Vatican library, one from a church at Obizine in France, and one from the cathedral library at Bayeux).[19] In later medieval times a compromise solution, chaining, was introduced. Stocks by this time were beginning to grow larger and therefore were difficult to control, and there is evidence of theft of illuminated works in order to steal the gold leaf.[20] The first chained library seems to have been at the Sorbonne in Paris in 1271, and the first in England in 1320 at St. Mary's College, Oxford.[21] Streeter, in his work on the chained libraries in England, lists twenty-nine libraries. Seven of them have never lost the chains, so we have extant examples, outstanding of which is the one at Hereford Cathedral. At Oxford, Magdalen was the last college to abandon chaining, and this as late as 1799.[22] But for the invention of moveable print, it is possible that chaining might still be practiced, but the increase in book stock which followed that invention made the practice less necessary and less practical. The protection of bookstock from theft is better served by a closed-access system which is both more economical and offers more protection since, before a reader acquires a work, it has to pass through the hands of a staff member, who can compile the necessary records of the transaction. The closed-access system was used by public tax-supported libraries until the end of the nineteenth century. They took the idea from previous library practice and were probably conscious of the dangers of allowing unlimited access. It was not until 1894 that open access was introduced at Clerkenwell in London by James Duff Brown, who two years previously had written an article on the subject entitled, "A Plea for Liberty to Readers to Help Themselves."[23] Prior to this, potential readers in a public library had to consult an indicator and/ or catalogue to help them choose stock. Ernest Savage, in his memoires, tells of irate readers who wanted to see books and how they were placated by junior staff, who laid a selection out on the counter for them. To quote, "Having learned how good it was to live among books and choose my own reading, I felt sorry for readers jammed before the indicator. Plainly we had to show books."[24]

In the early days of open access, there were a few libraries which reverted back to closed access, but they were a minority in a movement which gained impetus until eventually all public-library lending stock, at least, was on open access. Some were slow to convert—Stirling in 1947, Lossiemouth in 1948, and Stornoway in 1951, to quote some Scottish examples.[25] The effects of open access in the public-library lending departments have repercussions on reference collections, modern opinion holding that more of the stock should be open access. Perhaps the outstanding example of this is the proposed new Science Reference Library, which will have a large proportion of its stock on open access. The Dainton Committee estimated its stock at twenty miles of shelving and recommended that 90 percent of this should be open access.[26]

The trend toward open-access stocks is thus a triumphant one, but sadly there has to be an important qualification. There almost certainly has been an increase in the theft of stocks, and this is especially the case at the present day. Always conscious of the possibility, librarians have tried numerous methods to cut losses. One after another they have all proved failures. The wicket-gate system could not detect the book in the pocket; radial systems of ranges of book stacks only provided a theoretical ease of surviellance, as do mirrors placed at presumably convenient points. The use of detectives as floorwalkers and janitors at control points has also proved less than successful. All of this has resulted in a partial return to closed access, and heavily pilfered stock is usually removed from open access. In college libraries, certain popular periodicals, oft-referred-to reference books, and standard textbooks are often protected in this way. The actual cost of the loss of items is sometimes small in economic terms, but the disadvantage of not having a particular part of your memory when it is required can cause more serious problems. Further efforts to find new methods of control are being investigated. The field of electronics has offered hope because it is now possible to "bug" items and guard an entrance with an electronic signal so that an item which is taken out illegally will set off an alarm signal. One might well view this as a twentieth-century chaining method. Unfortunately, no system is yet perfect. For instance, unless an electronic guard is put on all windows—a costly operation—they must be kept shut or there is an escape route. Some libraries which have installed systems have reported reductions of losses. At Minneapolis, Minnesota, the following statistics have been reported:

Losses
Out of 5,104 issues of periodicals, 124 missing over 2 years
Out of 7,775 book requests, 929 missing over 1 year
     Calculated cost, $15,000 per year.
Annual cost of installations of theft-detection system, $11,000.

Effect
82% drop in book losses
72% drop in periodical losses[27]

It is not too much to expect that, in the near future, a system which cannot be compromised will be found so that larger libraries, at least, will have a method of protection which will allow them to have as much open-access stock as is necessary on a cost/benefit basis. It is too much to expect, although one is always hopeful, that there will be a return to a greater social consciousness, which might considerably cut losses.

It is to be hoped for, however, because, on the whole, libraries have always been eager to see that the greatest possible access is allowed to their stocks. If they are forced to introduce methods which in any way limit access, this can only be regarded as socially retrogressive.

NOTES

1. Young, O. R., "A Survey of General Systems Theory," in *General Systems,* vol. 9 (Society for General Systems Research, 1964), pp. 74-75.
2. Ibid., p. 74.
3. Johnson, E. D., *History of Libraries in the Western World,* 2nd ed. (Scarecrow Press, 1970), p. 141.
4. American Library Association, Library Administration Division, *Access to Public Libraries* (Chicago, 1963), p. xi.
5. Taylor, L. E., *South African Libraries* (Bingley, 1967), p. 39.
6. Luckham, B., *The Library in Society* (Library Association, 1971).
7. Ibid., p. 27.
8. Ibid., p. 77.
9. Groombridge, B., *The Londoner and His Library* (Research Institute for Consumer Affairs, 1964), p. 70.
10. Hoggart, R., *The Uses of Literacy* (Penguin, 1962), p. 250.
11. Great Britain, House of Commons, Sessional Papers, *Report from the Select Committee on Public Libraries, Together with the Proceedings of the Committee* (Her Majesty's Stationery Office, 1849), pp. 20-21.
12. Great Britain, Scottish Education Department, *Standards for the Public Library Service in Scotland* (Her Majesty's Stationery Office, 1969), Appendix C, p. 48.
13. Great Britain, Department of Education and Science, *Report of the National Libraries Committee* (Her Majesty's Stationery Office, 1969), p. 15.
14. Great Britain, University Grants Committee, *Report of the Committee on Libraries* (Her Majesty's Stationery Office, 1967), p. 119.
15. Ibid., p. 119.
16. Ibid., p. 118.
17. Great Britain, Department of Education and Science, Library Advisory Councils for England and Wales, *Public Library Service Points: A Report with Some Notes on Staffing* (Her Majesty's Stationery Office, 1971), pp. 14-15.
18. Great Britain, University Grants Committee, *Report of the Committee on Libraries,* p. 121.

19. Clark, J. W., *Care of Books* (Cambridge University Press, 1901), p. 30, Figs. 17, 26, 27.
20. Thompson, J. W., *The Medieval Library* (Hafner, 1967), p. 629.
21. Ibid., p. 625, and Streeter, B. H., *The Chained Library* (Macmillan, 1931), p. 4.
22. Streeter, *The Chained Library*, p. xv.
23. Aitken, W. R., *History of the Public Library Movement in Scotland to 1955* (Scottish Library Association, 1971), p. 192.
24. Savage, E., *A Librarian's Memories* (Grafton, 1952), pp. 67,71.
25. Aitken, *History of the Public Library Movement*, p. 194.
26. Great Britain, Department of Education and Science, *Report of the National Libraries Committee*, pp. 20, 87.
27. Huttner, A. H., "Measuring and Reducing Book Losses," *Library Journal* (February 15, 1973), pp. 512-513.

12

The Retrieval Problem

Open access in libraries greatly facilitates the retrieval of information and knowledge by encouraging browsing, a method not to be despised. Admittedly, it lacks the more purposeful approach of looking for a particular unit of stock, either by author, because you have been so referred to the work, or by subject, because this is your particular area of interest. But the very nature of the logic of these two approaches may be inhibiting in the use of a stock of a library. Open access, especially if the different sections are well labeled, gives the user the possibility of alighting on an approach to knowledge of which he has not thought; it may help the interdisciplinary approach to problems which are so common in this era of specialization and which are not reflected in the classification systems used by libraries. It may also help in effecting the association of ideas which is essential to the inventiveness of man; it aids spin-off from one subject field to another. Users of libraries seem to sense subconsciously the possibilities by showing their desire to browse.

The one disadvantage of browsing is that it contains a large element of luck, and the more serious scholar and researcher is going to use it only occasionally; as a rule he will find a prescribed item via knowledge of its author or its subject; it is to help this approach that libraries have provided catalogues and indexes of their stocks. Strictly speaking, a catalogue need only note the existence of a work in a collection without specifying where it is to be found; it becomes an index when location symbols are added. There is evidence that catalogues have always been part of larger libraries.

The clay-tablet library of Assurbanipal had finding-lists on a wall near the door. Callimachus, the renowned librarian of the Alexandrian Library, compiled a catalogue which has been estimated to have extended to 120 rolls. Roman libraries continued the practice, and the larger libraries of the Byzantine and Moslem empires have examples, as do the monastic and early university libraries.[1]

Thus, long before the great growth of libraries after the invention of moveable print, the necessity of compiling catalogues, even if some were inventories rather than finding-lists, is well established. The outstanding example is from the Alexandrian Library, which had a classified cata-logue which followed the shelf arrangement. It was known as the *pinakes* "tablets" and referred to the guides above the *armaria* ("book chests"). These guides carried a list of authors within the particular division of knowledge held in this cupboard. The total number of divisions is un-known, but some examples are *Oratory, Laws,* and that headache of all classifiers, *Miscellanea.*[2]

Comparatively speaking, the catalogues of early libraries were probably just as efficient as those of today. It was relatively easy to list the total stock of a pre-moveable-print library, and even up until the nineteenth century it was possible to keep up with the book stock, although the in-take of pamphlet literature created problems. An example of this is the collection of Thomason Tracts, collected between 1640 and 1661 and passed to the British Museum in 1762; a published catalogue was not pro-duced until 1908.[3]

It is, however, the nineteenth-century escalation of print, not to men-tion the influx of nonprint media, which creates real cataloguing prob-lems in terms of keeping abreast with the influx of new stock. The situation has been most critical in national reference libraries. The British Museum's first catalogue, in two volumes, was produced in 1787. It contained no press marks. A new edition in seven volumes was compiled between 1813 and 1819. In 1825 an attempt was made to produce a classified catalogue, but this had to be abandoned in 1834. The Committee of Inquiry into the Affairs of the British Museum in 1835-1836 recommended the updating of the catalogues, and in 1838 the trustees instructed Sir Anthony Panizzi, Keeper of Printed Books, to make and print a catalogue. In 1839 he pro-duced the famous ninety-one rules of cataloging which were from then on applied to the construction of the British Museum catalogues. By 1850, 150 volumes of a Guard Book Catalogue were completed, and by 1880 this had increased to 3,000.[4] Between 1881 and 1900, ninety-five volumes of a printed catalogue were produced which included all volumes in the Museum up to 1881. Between 1900 and 1905, it was found necessary to publish a supplement of thirteen volumes, covering the period 1882-1899.[5] Its successor is the prime example of the difficulties of producing printed catalogues. In 1931 a new edition was begun, but twenty-three years later, in 1954, it was left incomplete, having reached only DEZW.[5] It was abandoned in favor of newer methods of production, and between 1959 and 1966 a 263-volume catalogue was produced. Even at this size it does not cover the whole of the Museum's collections.[6] It covered up to 1955, and further chronological supplements have been necessary.

This brief outline of the problems of cataloguing in the British Museum is indicative of what was happening elsewhere. Very few catalogues covered the totality of stock; new ventures, such as the union catalogues of the Regional Library Bureaus, were to get further and further behind in attempting complete coverage; many public libraries abandoned catalogues in their branches, reasoning that on a cost/benefit basis they were not worth their compilation and upkeep time; and the new National Lending Library of Science and Technology (NLLST) announced that it was not going to catalogue its stock but to rely on published bibliographies and a simple alphabetical arrangement on the shelves.[7]

The pessimistic nature of the above comments is not to deny the very great use to which catalogues were put. On countless millions of occasions, users of libraries must have benefited from them in being guided to the works of their choice. In particular, the printed catalogues of libraries have been put to full use by other libraries in helping to trace the existence and descriptions of works they do not stock. They have played a fundamental role in bibliographical control. But there always have been very considerable problems which librarians must ponder and a large amount of research has been directed to these problems. As a result of this research there is hope, based on the application of the computer as a high-speed processor of information. The basic problem has really been one of finding the resources to cope with the volume of work rather than a problem of a deep intellectual nature, although such problems do exist in subject cataloguing, of which more later.

In the report on the application of automatic data processing (ADP) to the indexing systems of the new British Library, we find the following recommendation:

ADP should be used for all current cataloguing; all catalogues (author, subject, etc.) should be produced by computer methods

in future . . . . The use of ADP would enable full advantage to be
taken of recommended standardisation of cataloguing practices,
save duplicate cataloguing of c30,000 items per year, speed cataloguing in the BML, solve current problems and delays in catalogue
outputs to be produced in future, and simplify external publication of catalogues.[8]

In the face of previous failures, this may seem overoptimistic, since there
is also hope of doing some retrospective conversion of existing catalogues
and of increasing coverage of nonbooks, but this is precisely the kind of
hope that our new tool, the computer, can give. By using it, libraries can
cope with any volume of cataloguing likely to be required.

Given the fact that the British Library can cope with its intake of stock,
there are considerable spin-off effects on other libraries. The British National Bibliography Ltd., (BNB), now the basis of the Bibliographical Services Unit of the British Library, has for some years researched the possibilities of machine-readable cataloguing. The MARC project, as it is called, is
capable of encoding bibliographical information onto computer input
software. It is possible to make duplicates of the software available to
other libraries, which if they have compatible hardware, can extract the
information they wish for their own purposes. The BNB research has been
closely connected with similar work conducted in the U.S. Library of
Congress, and a high degree of standardization has been found possible.[9]
Despite many problems of compatibility, standardization, and time lag,
when one considers the short space of time spent researching this problem,
it must be conceded that the future is bright. If, from a central source, the
majority of cataloguing information required by a library can be supplied
quickly, and if the format is such that information, as required by a particular library, can quickly be selected from the master, then we have gone
a long way to solving the problem of volume cataloguing.

In the future, the major problem to be overcome in indexing is how to
deal satisfactorily with the subject approach to knowledge.

There are problems of author approach, but they are comparatively
minor. They consist mainly of the cataloguer supposedly having to make
a decision as to which author, from alternatives presented by a particular
book, he will choose for the heading for the main entry. It can be argued
that it is of no great import which one is chosen, since all alternatives
must have added entries and, in the days of simple duplication of entries,

it is possible to give full information on all entries. This is a slightly glib
argument since it views the catalogue as an indexing device for one particular item. The reader who wishes to find all works by an author will want
them all together in the catalogue, and if he finds some works under
"D'Israeli" and others under "Israeli,D." he is subjected to confusion
despite cross-references or added entries. The example is one quoted by
Edward Edwards as being the practice of the British Museum.[10] It was to
overcome problems like this that the Panizzi rules were compiled and, for
that matter, all other codes of cataloguing rules. In the interests of standardization, it is best to lay down rules and principles which will guide the cataloguer in creating uniform headings under which the user of the catalogue
is most likely to look. A similar problem exists with titles of works which
are likely to be cited in different ways, such as *Hamlet* and the *Arabian Nights.*
There are thirty-six columns of entries under *Hamlet* in the British Museum
General Catalogue of Printed Books, listing approximately 440 works, 140 of
which are translations with foreign titles. Some codes of rules have been compiled on a national basis, and one set is applied on a cooperative basis by the
United Kingdom and the United States. These Anglo-American Codes of 1908
and 1967 went a long way toward standardizing practice in the English-speaking
world, despite the fact that in both editions alternative rules had to be
printed because of the inability of those countries to agree on certain points,
and despite the fact that probably the majority of libraries made further
modifications for reasons of their own. The adoption of the rules by centralized cataloguing agencies has led to a much higher degree of standardization. Not only do these rules offer guidance for the compilation of
author catalogues; they also create models for the presentation of a description of an item, an area which also creates a number of minor problems of an intellectual nature and a major one of time consumption. These
can be overcome by centralized cataloguing and with ADP software, allowing selection of parts of a description by an individual library.

It is, however, the subject approach to information and knowledge
which is the more difficult from an indexing point of view. The problem
has to be looked at on two levels: the indexing of the "total subject" of
an item in the stock of the library, and the indexing of the specific subjects contained within each item. Coping with the first problem is mainly the province of librarians, coping with the second is mainly the province of the producer of the item. The qualifying word "mainly" is necessary because librarians do introduce an element of analytical cataloguing,

particularly in the case of periodical literature, and in some instances they have to compile indexes to material which has been left unindexed by the producers. This can be done for local newspapers.

As we have noted in the case of the *pinakes* of the Alexandrian Library, the subject approach to knowledge was recognized from earliest times, and some libraries arranged the stock itself, and also the catalogue entries, in a subject order. Divisions of knowledge were conceived of in broad terms and sufficed for the arrangement of the relatively small stocks of early libraries. The growth of knowledge, first spurred by the Renaissance and later by the Industrial Revolution with its implications for science and technology, led to degrees of specialization of knowledge, which in turn meant more and more specific methods of indexing. It is this growth which has created the need for research by librarians into their indexing methods.

At the British Museum, the first subject catalogue was planned in 1825 but abandoned in 1834. In giving evidence to the Committee of Inquiry of 1835-1836, Panizzi said that the greatest men of all centuries had talked about classified catalogues as a matter of theory, and that he thought it impossible to make a good classified catalogue.[11] His opinion proved correct at the time and it was not until 1881 that a subject catalogue was begun concurrently with the preparation of the *General Catalogue*. This is an alphabetical subject catalogue, not a classified one (as we would understand the term today). The entries in it are arranged alphabetically under the words chosen to describe the subject content, not under a notation which, in replacing the words, leads to a more systematic or classified arrangement. The first three volumes of the *Subject Index of Modern Works Added to the Library* were published between 1881 and 1900, and thereafter followed at quinquennial intervals. This is one of the earliest of the modern subject catalogues. Other examples are at Birmingham Public Library (1869) and Liverpool Public Library (1872). It is claimed that Charles A. Cutter traced the origins of the dictionary catalogue in the United States back to 1815. If Cutter himself laid no claims to be the originator of the dictionary catalogue, he was the first to lay down rules whereby their construction could begin to cope with a subject approach to the contents of a library. The first edition of his *Rules for a Dictionary Catalogue* was published in 1876, and by 1903, for a further two editions, total sales had reached 35,000 copies, leading to a fourth edition in 1904.[12] This is evidence of the interest in subject catalogues at this time and also of the validity of Cutter's approach. The catalogue he produced between 1874 and 1882 at the Boston Atheneum was the proving ground for his rules. Cutter's major contribution to subject cataloguing was his insistence on subject entry under the specific subject of a work, linking this to its more general heading by means of a cross-reference from the general to the special. He was the first to recognize clearly that in an age of specialization, specific, not general, subject headings were needed. He claimed that the rule of direct specific entry was the main difference between a dictionary and an alphabetically classed catalogue.

The concept of specificity occupied much future research in indexing. An example of an index compiled on principles of specificity is the London library's *Subject Index.* In comparing it with the British Museum *Subject Index,* one writer noted that "the London Library index is the easiest to consult, for it uses more specific headings and is adequately supplied with cross-references; that of the British Museum uses some awkward headings."[13] A similar remark could well have been made in comparing the British Museum *Catalogue of Printed Books.* compiled on principles of Panizzi's ninety-one rules, with any other catalogue formed on the principles of the Joint-Code Rules or the U.S. Library of Congress rules, which specifically ignore awkward composite headings such as *Academies* or *Periodical Publications.*

If the British Museum was reluctant to change its methods to meet the new rules of specificity, the U.S. Library of Congress was not. Congress started printing its catalogue cards for its own use in 1898 and in 1901 began to sell them to other libraries. The influence of its methods covered national and international ground. Cutter, in the preface to his fourth edition, paid tribute to its standards of cataloguing and, while noting some differences from his own rules, he recommended that libraries, particularly new ones, adopt its catalogue cards and thus most of its principles of cataloguing.[14] The pragmatic testing ground of acquisitions by the Library of Congress has ever since given invaluable service to author and dictionary cataloguing. Despite the preeminence of this catalogue as an example of a dictionary compilation, it was not until 1950 that the Library of Congress chose to publish a printed subject catalogue. Since the catalogue is in no way comprehensive of the total stock, entering only those books published since 1945 and catalogued since 1950, the magnitude of the task of compiling catalogues is still present even in the world's most wealthy library.[15] The work is updated by quarterly, annual, and five-yearly cumulations.

While the United States, under the influence of Cutter and the Library of Congress, is developing dictionary catalogues, the United Kingdom is opting more often than not for a classified catalogue, that is, one in which main (and some added) entries are arranged in a classified file according to a sequence of notation as supplied by a classification scheme. To this is added a subject index to the classified file.

The separate development of these two forms of catalogue has led to quite an academic battle, the exponents of the dictionary catalogue claiming that it is the easiest form to use, believers in the classified catalogue claiming that its systematic arrangement provides a much more valuable bibliographical tool. The debate is one which is not completely resolved, and the essence of the difference between the two forms may be seen in comparing two national bibliographies, the British National Bibliography (BNB) as a classified arrangement and the Cumulative Book Index (CBI) as a dictionary.

The development of classified catalogues has generated a great deal of research into the construction of classification schedules.

The early published schemes of Dewey (1876), Cutter (1891-1893), the Library of Congress (1904), and Brown (1906) were in competition for adoption and the winner was Dewey's, at least in public libraries. This was partly because it was first in the field, partly because he stabilized and made few changes after the second edition, partly because of a simple notation, and eventually because of a desire to standardize. All four schemes were severly criticized on the theoretical ground of a bad collocation of subjects. Dewey's no less than the others. But the pragmatists among librarians defended Dewey with the simple claim that it worked and that, on any cost/benefit basis, it was madness to think of changing from Dewey's to another scheme. This is why the later schemes of Bliss and Ranganathan, both based on sound theoretical grounds and both providing better collocations of subjects, have had very little practical success although their influence, particularly that of Ranganathan, has been considerable. Despite the fact that both schemes have effectively been rejected in practice, paradoxically, they are quite different. Bliss's is traditionally an enumerative scheme, almost all classes being listed in the schedules with only a little synthetic building of classes to be left to the classifier, and Bliss placed considerable stress on the simplification of notation. Ranganathan, on the other hand, introduced a completely new approach: the construction is according to facet principles and there is little enumeration of subjects, the classifier being left to construct his classes by joining together isolated concepts from different facets, a process which inevitably complicates notational problems. Ranganathan added to such problems when he insisted that notation be structured. This resulted in his scheme's providing a very complex notation, despite his efforts to prove otherwise, and this was one of the major reasons for the nonadoption of this scheme. Bliss, however, had a relatively simple notation and was still eschewed, so the main reasons for the retention of Dewey must be those outlined above.

Although Colon Classification remained unadopted, it provided an excellent theoretical model on which to experiment. The faceted principle has been adopted by other special classification schemes, one such example being the CRG scheme for Library Science, a scheme adopted by some libraries of library schools and the library of the British Library Association. Others, familiar with the Dewey arrangement, remain satisfied with it.

CRG are the initials of the Classification Research Group of London, formed in 1952. The products of its work are considerable, yet it has never achieved its original objective of preparing a new general classification system according to faceted principles, although a number of specialized schemes have been tried and found relatively satisfactory.[16]

The failure to produce a new general classification system has been caused by one apparently unsurmountable difficulty. This is the fact that a classification scheme may have two objectives, the arrangement of physical items and the arrangement of concepts, that is, either for the arrangement of books or shelves or the arrangement of entries for them in catalogues and indexes. It is now claimed that the more sophisticated a scheme is for the second objective, the less value it has for the first.[17] The proving ground for this work has been the BNB, which for the purposes of the arrangement of its own entries had to create sophisticated modifications of the Dewey system, which in turn created problems for those librarians who used BNB as a centralized classification agency to find ready-made class symbols for the arrangement of their stock. So severe have these problems been that BNB has now ceased to add its modifications and strictly applies the eighteenth edition. The wide use of the Dewey system by librarians pragmatically forced its adoption by BNB, although in the *British Catalogue of Music,* a new faceted CRG scheme is used.

The most fruitful result of research to date appears to be the development of the PRECIS indexing system. PRECIS (Preserved Context Index System) evolved from researches by the Classification Research Group, particularly in relation to MARC, and pragmatic testing in the laboratory of the BNB.

The alphabetical subject index to the BNB classified sequence of entries was originally compiled according to principles of chain indexing as propounded by Ranganathan. It is not too much to claim that in its five-yearly cumulations, this index proved to be the finest ever compiled for a classified file. Despite this, it had its limitations. The principle of chain indexing is applied best in practice if it is derived from the terms and structure of a faceted classification scheme. Since BNB is based on the Dewey system, an enumerative scheme, this created problems. In any case, it is best that a central agency supplies natural language terms independent of a particular classification scheme, since its users may be applying different schemes and it is possible for the central agency to supply various class notations.

Investigation into this, coupled with the necessity of producing machine-readable entries for machine retrieval, led to the development of PRECIS, a system which has been described as follows:

> It allows a user to enter the alphabetical index under any of the significant terms which make up a subject statement, and establish at that point the exact context in which his chosen term has been considered by the author. A summary statement—a kind of precis is found.[18]

The BNB has been produced from a machine-readable data bank since 1971. We still have to see a five-yearly cumulation of PRECIS indexing; there is every reason to presume that it will produce an even better subject index.

The development of recent research in classification has indicated two main trends, one new and one old. The new is that whatever methods one employs at the present time, every effort has to be made to make them machine-compatible, and this effectively means computer-compatible since only a computer is apparently capable of handling the quantity of work. The old is the basic problem of how to designate subjects, and this resolves itself finally into the fact that there must be a first-rate alphabetical sequence of sought words, if only as an index to a classified file. If it seems redundant to use the phrase "sought words," it might be prudent to note that an early university library arranged entries for its stock under the first word on the second page regardless of what that might be.[19] On what conception it was felt that this would be "sought" must remain one of the mysteries of the human mind.

It was the analytical mind of Ranganathan which separated the three planes of work on classification problems. There was the idea, or conceptual plane, on which the work was in the abstract; the notational plane, which demanded that the concepts which were isolated were allocated symbols so that when they were arranged by these symbols, they were in a helpful order of collocation; and the verbal plane which is of the greatest practical value since a considerable majority of readers approach the concept of a subject by labeling it with some form of natural language.

The basic problem is that the description of a relatively complex subject in true natural language may require a few sentences, if not a paragraph. This is too cumbersome, and so the indexer is faced with the problem of reducing the length of the statement while retaining the meaning, and arranging the words so that they can be filed under "sought headings." He either does this, precoordinating the terms which have to be used as subject designators, or he isolates the terms and leaves the user to bring them together in his use of the index—a postcoordinate system.

PRECIS at the moment is one of the most advanced of the precoordinate systems.

Uniterm, or single-term indexing languages, also have their vogues. In 1966 a research project concluded, "Quite the most astonishing and seemingly inexplicable conclusion that arises from the project is that single-term index languages are superior to any other type."[20]

In single-term indexing, the subject context of a document is analyzed into a number of terms, each of which might be sought by a user. The document is given a location number and this number is cited under each of the terms, but it is necessary for the user to bring the terms together and search the listed location numbers to see if the same one is under each term; if it is, that document contains the subject he is looking for. The following example may explain better the difference between the methods. If the subject content of a document is British government action in the fuel crisis of 1973, in PRECIS precoordinating indexing, the following entries would be made referring to this document:

GREAT BRITAIN
    Fuel Crisis, 1973. Government action
FUEL CRISIS. Great Britain, 1973.
    Government action.
GOVERNMENT. Action in Fuel crisis. Great Britain, 1973.

Further references, such as "ENERGY *see also* FUEL," would be needed to cover all possible sought headings. A full range of entries like this allows for all possible approaches to the subject— either to a specific definition, a more generic heading, or to a related subject.

In uniterm indexing, the document number would be cited under the following terms:

GREAT BRITAIN
1973
FUEL CRISIS
GOVERNMENT

All terms used in a uniterm system are carefully controlled by compiling a thesaurus which acts as an authority file and contains necessary cross-references.

Which system is used to designate subjects may well depend on the type of user and the subject- fields covered. For serious users who are capable of coping with postcoordination, there are advantages in the indicative nature of that system, whereas for the more casual approach, there are advantages in the more informative nature of the precoordinated statement. Derek Austin advances the thesis that some subject fields are "hard" in the meaning of terminology while others are "soft." In "hard" areas, where meanings are more precise, postcoordination is possible, but in "soft" subjects the precoordinate contextual statement is more helpful.[21] However true this may be, one must conclude that all indexing systems must be an optimization of a situation: the system must attempt to give a precision to natural-language statements which in themselves are often much less precise and much more verbose.

The conceptual approach of systems theory is also being noted by researches in indexing. For instance:

> Whatever the field to which a heading relates, it always follows a
> consistent semantic organisation. A term denoting an end-product
> takes precedence over a term denoting activity leading up to or
> acting upon that end-product, and if there is an agent concept
> involved, a term for the agent follows that of the activity . . . .
> A term in a string denoting a 'whole system' precedes one deno-
> ting part of a system.[22]

> Further work will proceed along the lines of combining inte-
> grative level theory with general system theory to produce a
> synthesis of facet analysis and relational analysis.[23]

> There are clear implications in this approach for the analysis
> of compound subjects, and since the techniques of system analy-
> sis have been applied successfully in a variety of subject fields,
> ranging from the hard to the soft end of the subject spectrum,
> the procedure would appear to have an obvious bearing on the
> design of a general classification . . . . The important point to note
> here is the special emphasis given to the role of the environment,
> which is seen as a concept whose principal function is to estab-
> lish the context in which a system is being considered.[24]

A further practical yet essential parameter has been added to the research problems in indexing. Not only must work proceed on the intellectual plane, but any system devised has to be machine-compatible.

Proof has already been given of the inability of librarians and biblio-
graphers to cope unaided with the bibliographical control of the world
output of graphics, and we have noted how ADP is to be applied to the
British Library and how the BNB is being produced from MARC tapes.
There can be no doubt that the work being done now is going to have
far-reaching implications on the future of indexing techniques.

For instance, the data on MARC tapes has been commercially available in the United States since 1968 and can be used by any library with
a compatible computer. There are many minor problems in their use, but
an experimental network of twenty-three libraries in the United Kingdom

has helped to isolate and cope with them, so that the BNB intends to convert back files of some 500,000 entries to machine-readable form on discs, which will allow random access, and the hope is that many of the new 115 local authorities in England and Wales will use this new data bank as the basis for compiling catalogues of their newly amalgamated stocks.[25] The success of this venture may well determine the validity of centralized MARC data banks. To get full benefit from the service, libraries must standardize their procedures to meet the data provided and the centralized service must allow as much flexibility as possible in the selection of the data it provides.

Given the success of the centralized service, there is every likelihood that more specialized indexes will be created at the local level, with at least the possibility of making the results of the labor more easily available. The indexing of archival material would be an example.

A recent work on the future of classification is almost entirely devoted to the effects and possible effects of mechanization, and one writer strikes the kind of futuristic note which is found more and more nowadays outside the realm of science fiction.

> Large-scale use of automatic classification techniques is probably
> at least a decade away. . . . We are on the way to demonstrating
> in a few years . . . that we can also teach computers to take over
> a portion of the intellectual analysis and classification of our record-
> ed knowledge, thus even reducing the need for our analytic skills.[26]

This certainly is possible in the hard subjects where sought words are likely to be used in titles or in abstracts, provided that these are fed into a computer, it can print out an alphabetical index, using these key words. The technique is already in use in the Key Word in Context (KWIC) indexing system, in which the key words are used to alphabetize entries but are printed in the context of the titles in which they appear.

Important as the compilation of library catalogues and indexes is, it is only one step to the retrieval of data from the memory store. Apart from a small percentage of analytical indexing, the majority of indexing is to a physical unit of information, for instance, a book or a gramophone record. There is a vital area of retrieval of specific information from the unit, and for this the units should be supplied with an index.

In precodex days, the indexing of works was almost unknown. This is surprising, yet understandable in that the *volumen,* or roll, was physically more difficult to index and, in any case, almost all were designed to be read continuously and little thought was given to future reference to particular parts of the text. Titles, if they existed, were nearly always at the end of the text.

> The lack of assistance to readers, or of aids to facilitate reference in ancient books is very remarkable. The separation of words is practically unknown . . . punctuation is often wholly absent . . . . It must also have been very difficult to find a given passage when required . . . . The convenience of the reader was little consulted.[27]

The codex format and its division of the text into pages slowly altered the situation. It was now possible to index the contents by providing headlines at the beginning of chapters, pages, and paragraphs and also in the margins or shoulders, collecting at least the chapter heads into a contents list. More modern techniques of headlining are shown in the use of the thumb, tab, or fore-edge indexes, their use being of particular value in works designed for reference purposes, such as dictionaries or directories.

Valuable as headlining is, it is very much second best to supplying a work with a full alphabetical index of its specific contents. The codex format was also most appropriate for this technique since reference could be made with ease to each leaf or page, and very few serious works are now produced without an index. Indeed, in the standard contract between publisher and author, there is a clause to the effect that the publisher can insist on the author's supplying "an index and/or a bibliography and/or an appendix . . . at the Author's expense." One major culprit in not supplying indexes is, unfortunately, the largest publisher in the United Kingdom, Her Majesty's Stationery Office (HMSO). One example of its lack of consideration in this service is a work which has been used in the preparation of this book, the Parry Report on university libraries. To be fair, there is a very full table of contents, but the following example will show how relatively poor a method this is. The Dainton Report on national libraries is a work very similar to Parry's, of almost equal size, with a full table of contents, and published only two years later, yet with a full alphabetical index. It takes a matter of seconds to determine that Dainton makes comments on the MARC project; it takes much longer to discover that the term is not used by Parry. In works which are supplied with an index, it is not

infrequently the case that the standard of indexing is poor and sought
headings which are in the text do not appear in the index. Thus, in searching J.A.C. Brown's *Techniques of Persuasion* for data I found that the
word "library" was not listed, yet in the text there is mention of the
influence of Mudie's circulating library. Nor is "Mudie's" indexed.
The omission can only partly be excused by the fact that the work is presented as a popular rather than a scholarly one. One cannot similarly excuse
J. W. Clark's *Care of Books.* Scholarly to the extent of being the standard
historical work on the subject, its index did not include the word "lock,"
despite its use in the text on page 30. In Margaret Burton's *Famous Liraries of the World,* there is a description of the fire at Strasbourg library.
The word "fire" is used as an index entry, but this incident is not indexed
because the words "goes up in flames" are used. There is no index under
"flames."

The author or compiler of a work can, of course, present his data and
ideas only in the particular sequence which he believes to be best for the
purpose of his particular re-creation of knowledge; the provision of indexes
caters to other approaches to information. Nowhere can this be better seen
than in the production of modern encyclopedias, such as *Britannica* or
Chambers. Both are self-indexing to the extent that the contents are arranged under an alphabetical sequence of headings, but both are also supplied with full supplementary indexes to guide readers to more specific
sought subjects which are not used as main headings.

A recent Penguin reference book, *Who's Who in the Ancient World,*
which is alphabetically self-indexing, still supplies a fuller index. The compiler, Betty Radice, begins her preface with the following apologies, "A
book on a subject like this can only be selective and perhaps idiosyncra-
tic, but this one has a full index."[28]

Despite the importance of indexes, it is only recently (1957) that the
Society of Indexers was formed. They form a joint committee with the
Cataloguing and Indexing Group of the Library Association and award
the Wheatley Medal for the most outstanding index over the preceding
three years. In 1969 the medal was awarded to James Thornton's *Index
to the Letters of Charles Dickens.*

It is this kind of source material which can be so valuable to the research
worker and yet so often lies unindexed. Such is often the case with local
newspapers, and it is appropriate to conclude this chapter by referring to
the problems of indexing these.

It can be taken for granted that the subject content of local newspapers is of considerable importance to the library store. We have noted how at the national level, the British Museum conserves all such publications, many out-housed at Colindale, and how public libraries have taken on the role of conserving libraries, at least so far as local history is concerned. A complete set of the local newspaper(s) would be considered essential to this collection, and many libraries have taken considerable trouble to complete their files. Most sets are bound into volumes and by way of further protection of the original, readers are often asked to use a microform copy. The really enthusiastic local historian can obtain his own microcopy from the British Museum if he wishes to pay for the service.

The public library may well make a catalogue entry under title for its local newspaper, and it may even add entries under editors and a form heading *Newspaper,* all of which could have their uses, though all members of staff should be able to answer the most likely question to be asked— do you have copies of the local newspaper? Apart from browsing through the files, the most frequent approach to the information in a local newspaper must be for specific subject data, yet it is precisely this which is left unindexed because of the apparent immensity of the task. It is sometimes true that the newspaper office itself will have some form of index, if only a self-indexing alphabetical sequence of clippings. But this is seldom the case, the journalists relying on their memory of the chronology of events to help them trace items, at least over the preceding few years, which may be all that they may want. The historian, too, may be to some extent guided by the chronology of events, but this approach may be unsatisfactory for an exhaustive search. To give a personal example, some years ago, in browsing in the Derby Public Library reference department, I suddenly became aware of the fact that the local newspaper, the *Derby Mercury,* had begun publication prior to 1745 and therefore probably contained accounts of the stay in the town of the Jacobite army of Charles Edward Stuart. Since I was not sure of the precise date in 1745, it took a little time to locate items in the weekly issues. An index would have helped, but more important was the fact that, without an index, I could not be certain that I had covered every item on the topic. Only a much fuller, time-consuming search could have determined this.

It seems that few libraries have attempted to compile such indexes. One recent source can give only four examples at York, Nottingham, Ealing and Chester.[29] At Nottingham the work had to be done by volunteers. A further example comes from the North Riding County Library, which held a coffee evening at which there were twenty-one volunteers to index the *Whitby Gazette.*[30] The division of labor is to be at the rate of four issues to each indexer, but in order to reduce the volume of work, value judgments on what information is likely to be sought or unsought are being made. Judging these judgments is interesting. To exclude chemists' opening hours seems reasonable on the basis of their being unsought; to exclude national and international news seems reasonable on the basis that the information is best found in national newspapers; but to exclude court proceedings and wedding announcements which could supply useful biographical information seems unreasonable. The inclusion of chemists' opening hours could be defended on the basis that some future researcher could find it of some significance in social history, and the inclusion of national and international news could be justified on the basis that it may be given a local slant

But it is only reasonable for an indexer to make value judgments on sought words, not on sought concepts, and the golden rule must always be, if in doubt, include, do not exclude. Exclusion is motivated by cost, not by possible benefit. Theoretically, the hope for the future must lie in the application of computers to automatic indexing because, if this should ever be achieved, it is doubtful that it would be worthwhile programming to make value judgments. It will probably be much more worthwhile to allow the machine a more or less free range and to accept the fact that there will likely be a number of unsought headings included. If they are unsought, who will ever know?

However, this kind of automatic processing is many years away, and we can only hope that automation of centralized services will reduce the work-load in individual libraries at the level of indexing units of stock, leaving to staff time available for indexing the specific contents within documents.

NOTES

1. Johnson, E. D., *History of Libraries in the Western World,* 2nd ed. (Scarecrow Press, 1970), passim.
2. Parsons, E. A., *The Alexandrian Library* (Elsevier, 1952), pp. 208-209.
3. Roberts, A. D., *Introduction to Reference Books,* 3rd ed. (Library Association, 1956), p. 132.
4. Rawlings, G. B., *The British Museum Library* (Grafton, 1916), pp. 160-161.
5. Roberts, *Introduction to Reference Books,* p. 78.

6. Great Britain, Department of Education and Science, *Report of the National Libraries Committee* (Her Majesty's Stationery Office, 1969), pp. 46,49.
7. Ibid., p. 106.
8. Great Britain, Department of Education and Science, *The Scope for Automatic Data Processing in the British Library* (Her Majesty's Stationery Office, 1972), p. xiv.
9. Great Britain, Department of Education and Science, *Report of the National Libraries Committee* (Her Majesty's Stationery Office, 1969), pp. 46, 49.
10. Rawlings, *The British Museum Library,* p. 152.
11. Ibid., pp. 147-161.
12. Sharp, H. A., *Cataloguing: A Textbook for Use in Libraries,* 4th ed. (Grafton, 1948), pp. 322, 313; Cutter, C. A., *Rules for a Dictionary Catalogue,* 4th ed. (Government Printing Office, 1904).
13. Roberts, *Introduction to Reference Books,* p. 75.
14. Cutter, *Rules for a Dictionary Catalogue,* pp. 5-6.
15. Roberts, *Introduction to Reference Books,* p. 73.
16. Foskett, D.J., "Classification Research Group, 1952-68," in Kent, A., and Lancour, H., *Encyclopedia of Library and Information Science* vol. 5 (Dekker, 1971), pp. 141-145.
17. Austin, D., "Two Steps Forward," in Palmer, B. I., and Austin, D., *Itself an Education* (Library Association, 1971), p. 70.
18. Austin, D.," Precis Indexing," *The Information Scientist* (September 1971), p. 95
19. Freeman, R. R., "Classification in Computer-Based Information Systems of the 1970's," in Maltby, A., *Classification in the 70's* (Bingley, 1972), p. 262.
20. Cleverdon, C., and Keen, M., *Aslib Cranfield Research Project: Factors Determining the Performance of Indexing Systems* (C. Cleverdon, 1966), p. 252.
21. Austin, "Precis Indexing," p. 100.
22. Coates, E. J., "Computerisation of the B. T. I.," in Houghton, B., ed., *Computer-Based Information Systems* (Bingley, 1972), p. 239.
23. Foskett, "Classification Research Group," p. 145.
24. Austin, D., "Trends Towards a Compatible General System," in Maltby, A., *Classification in the 70's* (Bingley, 1972), p. 239.
25. "Open Entry" (Announcements, reports, etc.), in *Catalogue and Index* (Summer 1973), p. 10.
26. Freeman, "Classification in Computer-Based Information Systems," p. 262.
27. Kenyon, F. O., *Books and Readers in Ancient Greece and Rome,* 2nd ed. (Clarendon Press, 1950), p. 69.
28. Radice, B., comp., *Who's Who in the Ancient World* (Penguin, 1971), p. 11.
29. Carter, G. A., *J. L. Hobb's Local History and the Library,* 2nd rev. ed. (Deutsch, 1973), p. 59.
30. North Riding County Library, *News No. 11* (November 1973), p. 2.

Part Five

THE EFFECT OF
THE SYSTEM

13
Reading

If, as in an open system, the output is connected to the environment, it is reasonable to assume that there is some change effected by the connection. As was noted in Chapter 1, in certain systems the nature of the change is such that it can be determined and often quantified, while in others one can only guess at what the change might be.

Only in the very crudest statistics of issues of stock and numbers of readers can the output of a library be measured. While it is possible to state that within a certain time period so many works were used by so many readers, and indeed it may be possible, therefore, to forecast with reasonable accuracy that a similar effect will take place in the forthcoming similar time period, this is purely a statistical quantification of the nature of the interaction between stock and readers and gives no real indication of any change which may have been effected in the reader or further changes which he may have effected on society at large.

It can well be argued that the crucial philosophical question to be asked about library systems is, "What change do they effect?" This is far from easy to answer in definite terms.

We have seen that living systems are goal-seeking if only in terms of a search for life-supporting nutrition. We have also seen, however, that man, when he became a tool maker, began to fashion his environment—initially to help sustain life-supporting nutrition but subsequently, when this became relatively easy with the development of agriculture and husbandry—to sustain life-supporting comfort, which, with the advancement of his technology, became more and more sophisticated. Even the general outline in Chapter 3 of the development of the communication systems which led to the establishment of libraries is sufficient to show the tremendous influence they had in helping man to seek and change his goals.

This is perfectly satisfactory as an explanation of the fact that libraries are effective in general terms and in the long term. There is no need to undertake empirical work to prove, at this level of understanding, the nature of the effect. By observation, we can say categorically that before the existence of libraries, society was in a certain state and that some 4,000 years later society is now in a radically altered state. When we add to this observation the fact that a very great deal of the change which has taken place, if not all, has been caused by the advance of one generation upon the knowledge of another, and that frequently this knowledge was obtained from the library store, then it follows that libraries have played a part, and possibly a large part, in effecting the changes. Whether the changes have been for the good or ill of society is a different question and, of course, one which is often asked in relation to the selection or rejection of materials for the library store. This may well be the ultimate question to be asked regarding the effect of libraries.

It is at this level that definitive answers become impossible because clearly, if one believes that present-day society is a disaster, then libraries have had a bad effect, but if one is content with the present situation, then they have had a good effect.

To return to an example previously used—the development of nuclear energy—it is easy to accept that this kind of technological advance could only have been made with the build-up of previous knowledge and, in many instances, by communication of this knowledge through libraries. It is understandable that some who deplore the military use of this force therefore conclude that libraries were, at least in this instance, an evil force, and that such is the magnitude of the evil that it overrules any good which may have been generated by libraries. To others, this is an extreme argument because it ignores the good effects and because it does not take into account other factors in a complex situation, that is, all the factors pertaining at the time when decisions were being made whether to drop the bombs or not.

Another view is that both of the above conclusions are wrong since they both make the assumption that libraries and their communications have been major factors in motivating mankind to good or evil when in fact they may only be minor factors in this respect. The argument is that communications from graphics are mainly effective in the transmission of information, data, and ideas, and whether these are used for good or evil is still a decision to be made by the individual. The decision he takes is motivated much more by the communications he has received directly from his fellowman. This argument does not deny that graphic communications are capable of arousing emotion, but it does maintain that there is much less likelihood of an overreaction to their stimuli than to stimuli received directly from another human. Looking at this argument more fundamentally, one is reminded of the proposition that man is an aberrant species, some evidence for which is to be found in the fact that it is only human beings who murder members of their own species. This is the essence of what we understand as evil, the immorality of murder usually being viewed as the worst. Theologians have proposed the doctrine of free will as an explanation: man has been endowed by God with the freedom of choice between good and evil. The fact is that man was committed to this behavior long before the existence of libraries. The archaeological finds of battle axes, common in Europe in the late Neolithic Age (i.e., c. 3000 B.C.), are evidence.[1] It is, in fact, reasonable to suggest that because of his aberration, man has created tools which he can put to a good or evil purpose as he wishes. Libraries are only one of the tools which he has created, and we can view them as a kind of secondary tool which helps to create the primary tools which do the real damage.

It is this latter line of thought which seems more acceptable, and it seems that most of the evidence of the effect of libraries bears this out. Before presenting the evidence and commenting on it, one important point should be made concerning methodology. This is probably best made by reference to the following quotation:

> The trouble started exactly when empirical research stepped in where once the social philosopher reigned supreme. To the latter there was never any doubt that first the orator and then the newspaper and now television are social forces of great power. But when specific studies were made about the effect of educational radio programmes or the influence of the library on the community, these facts could only rarely be demonstrated.[2]

The evidence which follows is a mixture of both types. There is comment on the effects of communications, reading, and libraries from social philosophers, taking that phrase to mean any competent person who has, from his own experience, something to say on the subject. There are also examples of some case studies and laboratory testing. Generally, the comments made by the social historians concern the long-term effects on society, those made by individuals concern the medium-term effects on themselves, and the experiments relate to the short-term effects on selected groups of people.

First, let us present commentary on the effect of communications and reading rather than libraries in particular, making the reasonable assumption that the comments could have referred to libraries, which could well have been the source of the reading.

On the general importance of communication to civilization, the historian Arnold Toynbee had no doubt about the essential effects:

> It can almost be taken for granted that a universal state will have
> provided itself with offical media of mental communication and
> that these will include not only one or more languages for spoken
> intercourse, but also some system of visual records based on a
> written notation.

He, as so many other historians, made no mention of libraries, but it can be taken for granted that he assumed their existence as a subsystem of the total communication system. Toynbee also had a pertinent comment on the nature of civilization:

> Civilisation might be defined as an endeavour to create a state
> of society in which the whole of Mankind will be able to live to-
> gether in harmony, as members of a single all-inclusive family. This
> is , I believe, the goal at which all civilisations so far known have
> been aiming unconsciously, if not consciously.[3]

The cynic might well remark that most of the endeavor has been at the unconscious level, but it must be conceded that a large and important part of communication is directed toward this end, yet paradoxically it can often have the opposite effect. The holy scriptures of the world have, taken as a whole, always attempted to promote the above ideal yet because of opposing doctrine in them, they propagated ideas which have led to many a holy war.

In more poetic, and thus more intense and effective comment, Marshall McLuhan paid tribute to the invention of writing:

The goose quill put an end to talk. It abolished mystery; it gave architecture and towns, it brought roads and armies, bureaucracy. It was the basic metaphor with which the cycle of civilisation began, the step from the dark into the light of the mind. The hand that filled the parchment page built a city.[4]

The juxtaposition of architecture and towns, and roads and armies, is indicative of our remarks about the use of any tool for either good or ill. McLuhan is a social philosopher, particularly in relation to social communications. He tends to take the overall, omnipotent view, and thus at times he overstates his case, yet his points are well made.

The intensity of the literary quotation ensures that the poet and writer of belles lettres is listened to, and it is not difficult to cull germane examples. The following have been sampled mainly from the *Penguin Dictionary of Quotations:*

It will create forgetfulness in the learners' souls because they will not use their memories; they will trust to the external written words and not remember of themselves. They will appear to be omniscient and will generally know nothing; they will be tiresome company, having the show of wisdom without the reality.

Socrates

This statement at least comes from someone who practiced what he preached. Socrates wrote nothing himself and it was left to Plato to record his thoughts and ideas. The fact that we still pay some attention to the Socratic method either shows the error of the statement, if it is accepted literally, or else it provides an excellent example of Socratic irony.

Books are good enough in their own way, but they are a mighty bloodless substitute for life.   *Robert Louis Stevenson*

This is a much more acceptable and shrewd remark which bluntly reminds us that books are a reflection of and a substitute for life and must be used with caution. This theme often occurs in quotations:

Deep versed in books and shallow in himself.   *John Milton*

The bookful blockhead, ignorantly read,
with loads of learned lumber in his head.   *Alexander Pope*

When a new book is published—read an old one. A man who attempts
to read all the new productions must do as the fleas do—skip.
                                        Attributed to Samuel Rogers

"What is the use of a book" thought Alice "without pictures
or conversations?"   *Lewis Carroll*

There are elements of truth in all these cynical observations, yet the
basic criticism implied is answered by:

Education . . . has produced a vast population able to read but
unable to distinguish what is worth reading, an easy prey to
sensations and cheap appeals.   *G. M. Trevelyan*

Whether the original motivation for human communication was utilitar-
ian or aesthetic, it was surely closely related to reality, and it seems reasonable to propose that the further a communication strays from reality, the
more likelihood there is of some danger to a receiver who believes that it
is reality. Later, there will be further examples of this blurring of reality,
which may be explicit or implicit in communication and may be intentional
or unintentional on an author's part. It seems to be essential that just as a
wild animal might teach its young to be suspicious of its environment because parts of it are likely to be hostile, mankind likewise should educate
its progeny to be critical of the communications they receive:

People say that life's the thing, but I prefer reading.
                                        Logan Persall Smith

This is the opposite view to Stevenson's, and while it may be attractive
to some, it is most appealing to the fanatic who is so immersed in his activity that he has lost sight of its original purpose. However, if one makes allowances for poetic license, it is indicative of how some think of reading.
Somewhat more balanced is:

I love to lose myself in other men's minds. When I am not walking, I am reading; I cannot sit and think. Books think for me.
                                        Charles Lamb

At least here, the reality of walking comes before reading, although "books think for me" is thin and counterbalanced by:

You, for example, clever to a fault,
The rough and ready man that write apace,
Read somewhat seldomer, think perhaps even less.
Robert Browning

Closer to a good approach is:

Be sure that you go to the author to get at *his* meaning, not to find yours. *John Ruskin*

or:

Choose an author as you choose a friend.
Earl of Roscomman

Read not to contradict and confide, not to believe and take for granted, nor to find talk and discourse, but to weigh and consider.
Bacon

These imply a critical approach. Perhaps the most apt and the most truthful of all is:

The reading of all good books is like a conversation with the finest men of past centuries. *Descartes*

It implies that books are merely an extension of talk, and since they are graphically recorded, they may be stored for the use of future generations. Their use is a two-way process between author and reader, both of whom have to apply themselves.

It is best to look at commentary on the effects of communications from people other than librarians, as librarians might well be accused of having a vested interest in showing that their system is effective and also effective for good. Nevertheless, making allowances for possible bias, here are observations by three librarians, chosen because of their reputations as bibliophiles:

Secluded from life, books lose life.

The study of mankind in literature and in the records of achievement belongs to the art of living. . . . Often we have no other
intellectual companions, or none so good.

Out of the few books I took all that I could. Some of them had
enduring influence. So education for good or evil, may be the
books near at hand, as I shall presently illustrate, that I have
always pled for *good* books in the home, the family open shelf.
My good books were few.   *Ernest Savage*

The first comment sustains the proposition that books must reflect
reality, the second that they can give access to the most profound thoughts
and ideas of all times, and the third that they can contain good and evil.

All reading, any reading is better than none.

There is nothing in daily work, in the most humdrum occupation,
that cannot be made more interesting or more useful through
books. They are a means to proficiency in every calling.

Consider what books may mean in individual development; in
the formation of character, in the activation of intelligence, in
the enrichment of resources, in the deepening of sensibility.
                                                    Helen Haines

The first obviously proclaims the author's bias and is a highly debata-
ble one. The second is more practical, another way of stating that books
can stimulate ideas. The third is more philosophical and presents the
case for the spiritual satisfaction to be had from books, the kind of
satisfaction found by our third librarian bibliophile. The following is
Henry Miller's comment on him: "The one person whom I found
satisfied with his lot, adjusted to his environment, happy in his work,
and representative of all that is best in the American tradition, was the
humble modest librarian at UCLA named Lawrence Clark Powell."[5]
Powell, more than any other librarian, has spent his professional life
campaigning for librarians to be bookmen first and managers afterward:

I am a practising bookman to-day because I was encouraged
to develop my basic bookishness, by my mother, my town librarian, two teachers at college, a printer and a book-seller, and
finally by a city librarian.

A natural devotion to books brings friendship with such different writers as Edgar J. Goodspeed, translator of the "New Testament", and Henry Miller, author of "Tropic of Cancer" both
of whom are prodigious users of libraries.

I am fortunate in being a rapid reader. Not as fast as T. E.
Lawrence, who of his years at Oxford said that he had read
every book in the library of the Union—the best part of
50,000 volumes probably.

"Where did it all begin" I asked [of his ex-school teacher].
"Right here in Delta" she replied. "When I was a little
girl in the public library—and I've loved books ever since,
excessively, unreasonably, passionately, yes and expensively.
I should have been a librarian and gone around spending
other people's money."   *Lawrence Clark Powell*

In each of these comments, Powell was referring to the impact made
on him by other book lovers, and this is indicative of most of his writing. He was, often as not, as much interested in the author as his works,
at least in the sense that behind all great literature there lie great minds
and, more often than not, a humanistic philosophy.

For evidence of the effect of books and reading on society at large,
one must search for the "impact" book.

Fortunately, this is very easy. An impact book is one which contains
ideas and attitudes which have been adopted by society and by which
society has been considerably altered. While no two persons would choose
exactly the same works for the compilation of a list, there is a fair consensus
of opinion of what might be included. One of the best lists available is the
catalogue of an exhibition of impact books held in London in 1963. Entitled *Printing and the Mind of Man,* the catalogue lists all the items of
printing mechanisms and printed materials put on exhibition at Earls
Court and the British Museum as part of the very much larger International Printing Exhibition (IPEX). The items on display at the Museum

mainly illustrated the aesthetics of printing; the Earls Court display held
the impact books.

There were 656 exhibits enumerated in the Earls Court Section, and,
as an estimate, 500 of these were books. The compilers commented as
follows:

> To demonstrate the impact of printing on the mind of man and
> the effect it has had on the history of the last 500 years . . . the
> task of reducing the mass of significant material to a representa-
> tive microcosm has been a harrowing one, even with the generous
> space afforded. . . . Examples [have been] limited to propagation
> of ideas.[6]

If it was difficult to pick 500 representative works, it is even more
difficult to choose a cross section of examples from them, but the following will at least serve as an hors d'oeuvre:

Philosophy			*Literature*
The Bible	Loyola	Dante	Defoe
St. Augustine	Bacon	Aesop	Chambers' Encyclopedia
Thomas à Kempis	Locke	Homer	
Plato	Bray	Malory	Encyclopedia Britannica
Luther	Kierkegaard	Shakespeare	Burns
Calvin	Ingersoll	Bunyan	Grimm
			Carroll

Science and Technology			*Politics*
Euclid	Fahrenheit	Gresham	Grotius
Hippocrates	Jenner	Wilberforce	Hobbes
Copernicus	Dalton	Erasmus	Paine
Mercator	Ohm	More	Smith
Galileo	Darwin	Henry VIII	Hansard
Napier	Mendel	Machiavelli	Owen
Newton	Einstein	Marx	
		Engels	

Art	*Travel*	*History*
Durer	Columbus	Herodotus
Ruskin	Marco Polo	Thucydides
Wagner	Hakluyt	Gibbon
Morris	Parkman	Carlyle
Le Corbusier	Livingstone	Grote
	Nansen	Macauley
		Toynbee

It would be a fascinating but massive study to trace the more detailed nature of the interaction that these works eventually had with society. Regretfully, we must accept the obvious that they did and only briefly comment. One example of the estimated effect of one of the writers is that "when the American Revolution came, it was made inevitable by the tyranny of printed laws; inspired by the printed philosophies of a bygone age, promoted by letter, newspaper and broadside; and fanned into flame by the publication of a single pamphlet: Thomas Paine's 'Common Sense.' "[7]

The broad classification of the short list is mine and the choice is more or less random, yet it shows fewer works on art. The reason for this is that the real impact of art is in the process itself rather than books about the process. It would be interesting to see the similar list of impact works of art.

It should also be remembered that "impact" is used to denote works of long-term rather than just immediate value. Occasionally a work was so poorly circulated that it received little attention until rediscovery at a future date. An example of this is the work of the monk Mendel, whose experiments on the cross-breeding of sweet peas in his monastery garden were first published in 1865 but were almost totally ignored until further work by William Bateson in the 1890s led to their reappraisal.

Perhaps a more pertinent example in the context of this work would be a more detailed list of the chosen works which relate to communications. An abstract of the annotation which is added to each of the entries in the catalogue is given:

Gesner, Conrad. *Bibliotheca Universalis.* 1545.
   ... first of the systematic "books about books"
   ... the beginning of all modern bibliography.

Index Librorum Prohibitorum. 1559.
   ... the classic example of censorship ...
necessary because of the invention of printing.

Milton, John. *Areopagitica.* 1644.
   ... magisterial defence of the freedoms of speech.
writing and printing ... "Give me the freedom to know, to utter, and to argue freely according to conscience, above all liberties."

Braille, Louis. *Procédé pour écrire au moyen de points.* 1829.
... perfected a system of embossed dots . . . completely successful and is now in almost universal use . . . Braille blind
himself.

Talbot, Henry Fox. *The Pencil of Nature.* 1844.

Daguerre, Louis Jacques. *Historique et description des procédés
du daguerréotype. 1839*
Priority of discovery (of photography) will be argued till doomsday
by the respective supporters of Niepce, Daguerre, and Fox Talbot.
The Englishman was unquestionably the inventor of the negative/
positive process which has completely superseded the French
invention.

Bell, Alexander Graham. *Researches in Telephony.* 1876.
Bell took out the first patent, which, though often contested was
upheld by the courts.

Hertz, Heinrich Rudolph. *Untersuchangen uber die Ausbreitung
der elektrischen Kraft.* 1892.
Investigating Clerk Maxwell's conception of light . . . Hertz
discovered that electricity could be transmitted and recorded
through space. This led to Marconi's perfection of wireless
telegraphy.

Marconi, Guglielmo. *Provisional Specification. Improvements
in Transmitting Electrical Impulses and Signals.* 1896.
First successful experiments in Bologna . . . granted a patent
in London in 1897 and GPO formed the Wireless Telegraph
Company, and in 1901 a trans-atlantic message was successfully sent.

Lumière, Auguste and Louis. *Notice sur le cinématographe.* 1897.
. . . the first to produce a practical machine with commercial
possibilities.

Fleming, John Ambrose. *Improvements in Instruments for Detecting and Measuring Electric Current.* 1904.
This is the invention of the thermionic valve which was adapted for wireless telephony in 1907 . . . it eventually made broadcasting feasible.

As with the works on art, there is nothing on the invention of printing as such in this list, the reason being that the impact of printing was made by the products of the process, and the techniques were passed on by apprenticeship rather than by the press itself. It was not until 1683 that the first handbook of printing, Joseph Moxon's *Mechanick Exercises,* was published. The impact of science and technology is very clear from the list, and there is clear evidence of how scientific discovery led to technological application, and of the build-up of experience from one impact to the other. Again, the general, if not the specific, effects of this form of communication are obvious.

The organizers of the exhibition had no doubts as to its importance. Clearly displayed at the entrance were the following words:

Here you will see the primitive tools that brought about a vast revolution in human thinking, as the printing press and moveable type opened new windows to knowledge in Philosophy and Religion, Science and Invention, Political Ideas and Social Theory. Here you may see how mechanical invention rose to the demands of the ever-widening literate public, and turned the handicraft of Gutenberg into the colossal industry which IPEX displays. Here you will find the original editions of books that have changed and expanded man's vision of himself and of his world through these five centuries.

And at the exit one was reminded:

Your journey through five centuries has brought you to this threshold. Now as you make your way out into the modern wonderland of IPEX '63, you come back to a world in which the spoken word as well as the written, can be infinitely multiplied. But printing will stand alone through the centuries to come as the gateway to the freedoms of the literate mind; the freedom to stop and ponder without losing the thread; the freedom to turn back and challenge any glib assertion at the start; the freedom to turn to the end and see whatever subtle intention it may reveal.

In this century printing has swept the light of literacy across whole new nations, beckoning new millions to responsible citizenship.

Before the year 2000, the entire human race will be reaching for the priceless gifts that printing brought to the mind of man.[8]

It would probably be most effective to conclude this general account of the effects of reading with reference to a specific case which is most likely to be indicative of the effect of many works although the final outcome is most unusual. The reader in the case was a young American convict, Frank Canisio, who, in his autobiography *Man against Fate,* related how he was strongly moved in reading one of Ralph Emerson's essays, "Self-Reliance." The philosophy behind the words, "Nothing can bring you peace but yourself. Nothing can bring you peace but the triumph of principles," made such an impact on his mind that he embarked upon twenty-three years of study, including law, and ultimately conducted his own defense at a retrial, after which he was freed.[9]

This is a classic example of the stimulus-response situation. Emerson's words must have been read by many thousands of people without this dramatic impact, yet Canisio was profoundly affected because he was basically motivated to do something to overcome his environment. The words supply the stimulus of an idea to a person in a receptive condition.

NOTES

1. Bray, W., and Trump, D., *The Penguin Dictionary of Archaeology* (Penguin, 1970), p. 36.
2. Smythe, D. W., "Some Observations on Communications Theory," in McQuail, D., *Sociology of Mass Communications* (Penguin, 1972), p. 23.
3. Toynbee, A., *A Study of History,* new rev. ed. (Book Club Associates, 1972), pp. 44, 296.
4. McLuhan, M., and Fiore, G., *The Medium Is the Massage* (Penguin, 1967) p. 48.

5. Miller, H., *The Air-Conditioned Nightmare* (Heinemann, 1945), p. 10.
6. *Printing and the Mind of Man: Catalogue of a Display* (F. W. Bridges and Sons, 1963), pp. 7-8.
7. Johnson, E. D., *History of Libraries in the Western World,* 2nd ed. (Scarecrow Press, 1970), p. 495.
8. *Printing and the Mind of Man: A Keepsake to the Exhibition* (1963) pp. 2,3.
9. Hannigan, M. C., "The Reader with Mental and Emotional Problems," *ALA Bulletin* (October 1964), pp. 798-803.

14
Pornography and Obsenity

Two areas of communication, more than others, have been subjected to a detailed analysis of their effect; one is advertising, the other pornography. Since the purpose of advertising is to sell a product and since advertising programs can be expensive, cost/benefit analyses are continually being applied. The fact that advertising continues on all media seems to prove that there is an effect, and advertisers feel that it is beneficial: "An understanding of the communication between individuals is essential for a full comprehension of the system." This quasi-law of systems theory noted in Chapter 1 has been applied in the advertising field.

Since the objectives of advertising are relatively simple and since the purpose of the vast bulk of advertising is to reach as many people as possible, it is necessary to construct the message in as simple terms as possible. What this amounts to is that the brand name of the product must be imprinted in the mind of the receiver, together with an image of the product and a motivation to buy the product. Psychology, as an organized and scientific study of human behavior, has shown that it is often the very basic needs of the human system to which it is best to appeal, even though the product one is trying to sell does nothing for this need. This is why one sees so much sex symbolism in modern advertising. It is not sufficient to convince a buyer that a motor car is an excellent purchase purely from the point of view of its basic purpose as a means of transportation; appeals are made to the violent nature of man in terms of the speed and acceleration of the car, and further appeals are made to his sexual drive by adorning the advertisements with the fair sex in an ever-decreasing amount of clothing. Such is the state of advertising that it would even seem that sex symbolism is found where it was not intended. One writer claims that the shape of cars is phallic and that the parameters of engine size and aerodynamics are not so important as one might think.[1]

It is no part of the purpose of a library to become a direct advertising agency for commercial products, although there are minor and occasional instances when they have accepted such advertisements in the form of bookmarks or dust jackets. As they stock works which contain advertisements, they become an indirect agent, and this will be part of the total effect. We can assume, however, that few readers will use a library for the specific purpose of consulting advertisements unless it be for research, and therefore it would be somewhat false if comment were made on the effect of advertising as if it were an effect of libraries.

It is much more relevant to investigate the effects of pornography since this is apparently part of the library store. There are many examples of the managers of libraries being concerned about its effects.

The preceding paragraph cautiously states that pornography is "apparently" part of the library store. Caution is indicated simply because it is usual, when discussing this subject, to attempt to define pornography and obscenity. However, under any definition, it is more than reasonable to claim that it has always been possible to find them in libraries. Pornography is derived from the Greek *porne* ("prostitute") and thus literally means "writing pertaining to prostitutes," while obscenity is derived from the Latin *obscenus* ("ill-omened"). Certainly, under these definitions the topics are well-represented in libraries. For the legal purpose of attempting to censor works of this nature, legislation in the United Kingdom defines an obscene publication as follows: "if taken as a whole . . . to deprave and corrupt . . . having regard to all relevant circumstances."[2] This definition is motivated by the fact that it is felt that there can be harmful effects from pornographic material. An even wider definition is suggested by a recent report. In presenting drafts for new legislation, it offers the following: "an article or performance of a play is obscene if its effect, taken as a whole, is to outrage contemporary standards of decency or humanity accepted by the public at large."[3]

All practicing librarians at some time or other must have received complaints from readers who have been outraged. The difficulty with the above definitions is highlighted by the observation of D. H. Lawrence that "what is pornography to one man is the laughter of genius to another."[4]

It is statements like this which make one stop and think more deeply about precise effects, although it is still implicit in the statement that effect is produced.

In practice, society has most often felt that the deleterious effect of obscene literature is to encourage the reader to violent and sexual acts. But some writers defend the literature of eroticism. The nature of this defense is well-expressed by one of the contributors to the above-mentioned report, David Holbrook:

If we look back at the past, we shall find that there has always been pornography—ranging from the most beautiful erotic art to public rape . . . . Various commentators have found that the primary dynamic of pornography is hostility and rage. By contrast eroticism tends to encourage love and consideration.[5]

This kind of comment takes us nearer to the heart of the matter. It is not the subject or topic which is in itself obscene but the manner in which it is handled. Also pornography is that writing which appeals to the baser instinct of violence in man, an instinct which the entire process of civilization has attempted to subjugate and which yet is commonly expressed. The failure of man to conduct himself in a civilized manner has naturally made him look for causes outside himself. As he looks at his environment, it is perhaps understandable that he should find as one of his scapegoats the communications he receives from others.

Because the comments of the social historians and writers are so contradictory, it is only to be expected that, in this age of scientism, we should turn to empirical research to attempt to prove the effects of pornography.

The fullest research conducted on the subject was that promoted by the Commission on Obscenity and Pornography, a committee which was established by the United States Congress in 1968 and which produced its published report in 1970. The committee was divided into a number of panels, each charged with an area of investigation. The task of one panel was to research the effects of pornography. The following quotations from the report summarize its conclusions:

There is no consensus among Americans regarding what they consider to be the effects of viewing or reading explicit sexual materials.

Surveys of psychiatrists, psychologists, sex educators, social workers, counsellers and similar professional workers reveal that large
majorities of such groups believe that sexual materials do not
have harmful effects on either adults or adolescents. On the other
hand 58% of police chiefs believed that "obscene" books played
a significant role in causing juvenile delinquency.[6]

These surveys support the view that an assessment of pornography
and its effects may depend on a particular person's viewpoint. It would
seem that the police chiefs, more than others, had to find a scapegoat
explanation. There is also some evidence that some psychiatrists do likewise: "Experimental and survey studies show that exposure to erotic
stimuli produces sexual arousal in substantial portions of both males
and females. Arousal is dependent on both characteristics of the stimulus and characteristics of the viewer or user."[7]

In essence, therefore, empirical research has proved the prima facie
case that there is an effect. The report further comments on the more
detailed results of the researches.

The basic conclusion that an effect occurs relates only to the emotional level. Further experiments revealed that while there was an emotional arousal, the majority of respondents claimed that this did not lead
to sexual action, a few claimed increased activity, and a few others claimed a decrease. There was an increase in dream fantasies. This seems to
sustain a proposition that the major effect of communication is on an
individual's mind, and some further stimulus is needed before the mind
causes the body to act. The initial emotional response can be strong but
short-lived.[8]

It was found that repeated exposure to sex-stimulus literature over
fifteen days reduced the level of arousal, although there was a partial
recovery of interest after two months. There was difficulty in finding
evidence to show that this type of reading changed attitudes, although
some respondents claimed that they became more liberal toward the
attitudes of others.[9]

The above findings prove only the erotic effect. It was found impossible to relate the reading of this literature to delinquent behavior. In
reporting this, the report refers to the Danish experience: when all forms
of censorship and control of printed materials were abolished in Denmark,
it was found that there was a subsequent drop in sex crimes. "In sum,

empirical research designed to clarify the question has found no evidence to date that exposure to explicit sexual materials plays a significant role in the causation of delinquent or criminal behaviour among adults or youths."[10]

It should be noted that one member of the commission, Charles Keating, the Chairman of the Citizens for Decent Literature, vigorously opposed the above evidence, claiming that the methodology was false and that the evidence of some experiments had been suppressed. It is certainly true that any method which relies on answers from people must be suspect since one can never be absolutely certain whether they are lying or telling half-truths, consciously or unconsciously.

After the American report was published, a somewhat similar investigation was begun in the United Kingdom by Lord Longford, and the result of this was published in 1972. The Longford Committee did not provide any further empirical research into the problem, but it did commission a survey of the research. This was conducted by Michael Yaff, and his conclusions are very similar to those above:

There is no consensus of opinion by the general public or by professional workers in the area of human conduct about the probable effects of sexual material.

Firm demonstrations of the damage done by pornography (or for that matter, of the benefits of any) are notoriously hard to come by. . . . This proposition is not likely to be disputed by anyone who, for example, has investigated the cause of crime . . . . Ambitious efforts were made in connection with the American Commissions on Obscenity, but . . . results were inconclusive.[11]

In this case, it must be admitted that much of the research looked at originated from the American inquiry, but nevertheless it provides an independent assessment. Once again, there are dissenting voices: David Holbrook and Mary Miles refused to accept the results of the empirical research, claiming that man and his behavior cannot be isolated clinically and examined in this fashion. In Holbrook's case, this seems somewhat ironic since the results seem to sustain his outlook. It can only be surmised that his opposition stems from his strong love of humanity and therefore a belief that it cannot be treated this way, and a reluctance to accept

evidence which suggests that the type of pornography which he abhors
is having little effect.

One chapter of the Longford Report is a review of a few individual
case studies submitted by volunteers.[12] The majority of these sustain the
case that the reading of pornography has bad effects, but the report is
fair in that it also gives examples which indicate that pornography was
of value to the impotent. Most of the examples beg further questions.
There is the case of a boy who found vicarious excitement in presenting
younger boys with pornographic material, but when one realizes that
this occurred within the environment of a boarding school, it may be assumed that the basic problem was not only with the pornography. There
is the case of the "religious and intellectually gifted" ex-prisoner who
was sexually deviant and also addicted to pornography. He claimed to
have been led to pornography by reading letters to a newspaper. This is
a classic example of pornography being in the eye of the beholder—the
letters were about corporal punishment at home. Another case is of a
young boy found hanged to death, with a popular paper open at the
photographs of half-naked females, one with a rope around her neck.
The report claims that this is not uncommon, and another work lists
twelve such cases.[13] All of the twelve cases concern young boys who re-
enacted dangerous scenes as depicted in comics, and the question begged
is, "What of the millions of others who read the same scenes and were
not affected in this fashion?"

There are also examples of delinquent behavior perhaps stemming from
nonpornographic works. "The boy who runs away, or 'takes-off' from
home, is of course, part of the romantic American tradition of Huckleberry Finn or of the classic success stories of self-reliant self-made men.
But the contemporary runaway makes a less romantic story—at least to
his parents." Thus writes a newspaper journalist in the middle of an article, headlined "Mass Murder Horrifies Parents of Runaway Children,"
reporting the beginnings of a trial in America at which the defendant
was facing charges of the murder of twenty-seven Houston boys, many
of whom were runaways. The inference is that *Huckleberry Finn* has
affected the culture of the United States to the extent that in the year
1973, 600,000 children ran away from home. It may be that literature
kindled the idea, but other environmental circumstances are more important factors, as the article goes on to say: "For he is often fired less
by ambition or love of wide-open spaces than by a sense of neglect and

despair at home and he may, paradoxically, be looking not so much for escape as for some sense of belonging."[14] Another example showing how literature stimulates ideas is given in an account of a bank robbery in London, August 1971. The thieves' haul was in the region of £1,500,000, and the prosecutor at the Old Bailey trial told the jury that the methods used were a copy of the Sherlock Holmes story *The Red Headed League,* the only difference being that in real life there was partial success, whereas in the story the thieves tunneled into the bank only to be met by Holmes and Watson.[15]

Because the emotions of the young are still in the process of stabilizing (and it is worth noting that none ever reaches 100 percent), it is natural that children and adolescents should be affected more than adults. Even among the strongest of anticensors, there is often a feeling that the young should be protected. The area of children's literature comes in for special examination in relation to its effects, in particular the cult of the comic, which has its basic communicatory appeal in the picture rather than the word. Nearly all investigators assume that there is an effect, and often a bad effect, and therefore they often produce some odd conclusions. It is possible for an adult to see bad in a very great deal of what appeals to children since one way of appealing to them is to invite them into a fantasy world in which they are gratified by the predicaments of other people. If these people are adults, so much the better, and if the predicament is caused by a child, with whom the reader identifies, better still. The much-loved Billy Bunter of yesteryear is a case in point. Certainly, most of the gratification in reading Bunter is derived from the fact that he is odd-man-out, a common game among children, and it is understandable that there should be objectors to this. It did, in fact, lead one well-meaning children's librarian at Ipswich to remove the Bunter books from open access, but, judging from the ridicule poured on this action by the press, the public at large was outraged by her action much more than by the Bunter stories.

It is the horror comic, however, which is apparently the much more potentially dangerous. One of the greatest condemnations of this type of publication is the work of Francis Wertham. Despite the claim of the American Commission on Pornography that surveys of psychiatrists showed that the majority felt that there were no harmful effects from pornography, Wertham in his book mounts a scathing attack on crime comics. The work is the result of seven years of scientific investigation.

Wertham, a senior psychiatrist dealing with delinquent children, became
convinced that the horror comic was a strong influence. He was particularly interested in mental hygiene and concluded that the horror comics
were a pollution of the mind. His definition of the crime comic is that
its basic ingredient is "violence, sadism and cruelty, and the superman
philosophy."

The statistics he gives for the increase of this cult in the United States
are of almost staggering significance. For the years 1937 to 1947, there
were only nineteen titles; between 1946 and 1947, they represented one-
tenth of the total output and by 1949, one-third; and by the 1950s, the
vast majority of comic output was of the crime variety. In 1948 the figure of issues per month is put as high as 75 million, one issue for every
two persons.[16]

There is no suggestion in Wertham's work that he opposes the subject
of crime as such in comic books, but he takes vilent exception to the methods of depiction. To give an example, he quotes from "a psychologist's
interpretation of a drawing made by a boy of a typical comic-book illustration of a pirate."

> This drawing is bristling with phallic symbols—the sword, the out-
> stretched arm, the big gun stuck under the belt, the conspicuous
> belt buckle and the shirt opened down to the belt; the way the
> legs are posed and the boots are drawn has some phallic quality
> too. The actual genitals are extremely accentuated. The figure
> is that of a very glamorous man, the looks seductive. The whole
> body is emphasised more than the head and there is very little
> attempt at control. This child was pre-occupied with sexual ideas.
> He is very aggressive sexually—not someone who would ask nicely,
> but who takes (rapes).[17]

A comment like this begs the question as to whether the symbolism
was seen by the psychologist while the boy was only copying what he had
seen without realizing its significance. Psychiatrists would argue that even
with a lack of conscious realization, a subconscious seed has been planted,
and they think that they see the results of its growth in the delinquent
cases they handle. Or at least some would. Wertham admits that some
of the crime comics are endorsed by psychiatrists, but he claims that at
best these psychiatrists are misguided and at worst they are fraudulent

because they have accepted substantial payments for their endorsements. Wertham's summing up is:

> The general lesson we have deduced from our large case material is that the bad effects of crime comic books exist potentially for all children and may be exerted along these lines.
>
> 1) The comic-book format is an invitation to illiteracy.
> 2) Crime comic-books create an atmosphere of cruelty and deceit.
> 3) They create a readiness for temptation.
> 4) They stimulate unwholesome fantasies.
> 5) They suggest criminal or sexually abnormal ideas.
> 6) They furnish the rationalisation of them, which may be ethically even more harmful than the impulse.
> 7) They suggest the forms a delinquent impulse may take and supply details of technique.
> 8) They may tip the scales toward maladjustment or delinquency.[18]

The wording of this conclusion is interesting in that it does not claim absolute proof but only a potential danger. The reason for this is surely that even Wertham's "large case material" is a minute sample of the total readership, and an obvious conclusion is that a very large proportion of the readership remains unharmed, and therefore that a small proportion of "harmed" cases in all probability had other environmental and perhaps hereditary influences acting upon them.

Wertham's warning was heeded, however, in the United Kingdom when in 1955 the Children and Young Persons (Harmful Publications) Act was placed on the statute book. This is described as "an Act to prevent the dissemination of certain pictorial publications harmful to children and young persons. "It cites these as "being stories portaying

(a) the commission of crimes: or

(b) acts of violence or cruelty: or

(c) incidents of a repulsive or horrible nature

in such a way that the work as a whole would tend to corrupt a child or young person into whose hands it might fall."[19]

The Act has been successful in keeping a great deal of horror-comic material out of Britain. In the year 1968-1969 some 800,000 magazines and 700,000 books were seized by British customs officials.[20] It would be very hard to sustain a case that the banning of horror comics has in any significant way reduced delinquency in the United Kingdom. There has been no great liberal outcry against the Act, an indication of the low value placed on the comics.

It seems clear, therefore, that when a person reads a book, looks at a comic, views a motion picture or television show, or listens to the radio, there is likely to be some immediate response which will vary in intensity from person to person, but in all instances the response is in the mind of the receiver, and it may be an intellectual or an emotional response. Whether the mind memorizes the initial impact and is so conditioned that it later leads the body to commit actions relating to the response is much more difficult to prove empirically, since one would need to have a full history of all messages received.

The situation is well summed up in one of the technical reports of the American Committee on Obscenity: "It remains clear that many men see and read large amounts of pornographic materials without any detrimental results. More attention needs to be paid to what innoculates persons against the potentially detrimental effects of exposure."[21]

A similar conclusion is found in a quite independent report which investigated the possible correlation between violence on television and delinquency:

> The whole weight of research and theory in the juvenile delinquency field would suggest that the mass media, except just possibly in the case of a very small number of pathological individuals, are never the sole cause of delinquent behaviour. At most, they may play a contributory role, and that a minor one.[22]

Now, therefore, the most that can be categorically stated is that there is an immediate emotional stimulus to the mind in reading pornographic or erotic literature, but only in a small minority of cases does this lead to physical action, either good or bad.

NOTES

1. Morris, D., *The Human Zoo* (Cape, 1969), p. 108.
2. Great Britain, Statutes, *Obscene Publications Act, 1959* (Her Majesty's Stationery Office, 1959), p. 1.

3. *Pornography: The Longford Report* (Coronet Books, 1972), p. 383.
4. Lawrence, D. H., *Pornography and So On* (Faber, 1936), p. 11.
5. *Pornography: The Longford Report,* p. 465.
6. United States, Congress, *The Report of the Commission on Obscenity and Pornography* (Bantam Books, 1970), p. 27.
7. Ibid., p. 28.
8. Ibid., pp. 28, 30.
9. Ibid., p. 28.
10. Ibid., pp. 30, 32.
11. *Pornography: The Longford Report,* pp. 101, 465.
12. Ibid., Ch. 6.
13. Wertham, F., *Seduction of the Innocent* (Rinehart, 1953), pp. 231-232.
14. Sampson, A., "Mass Murder Horrifies Parents of Runaway Children," *The Observer* (January 13, 1974).
15. *Scotsman* (January 3, 1973).
16. Wertham, *Seduction of the Innocent,* pp. 29-30.
17. Ibid., p. 77.
18. Ibid., p. 118.
19. Great Britain, Statues, *Children and Young Persons (Harmful Publications) Act, 1955* (Her Majesty's Stationery Office, 1955), p. 1.
20. Church of England, General Synod, Board for Social Responsibility, *Obscene Publications, Law and Practice* (Church of England, 1970), p. 8.
21. United States, Congress, *The Report of the Commission on Obscenity and Pornography* (Bantam Books, 1970), p. 30.
22. Halloran, J. D., and others, *Television and Delinquency* (Leicester University Press, 1970), p. 178.

15

The Library Contribution

In investigating the effects of reading in the preceding two chapters, it has been mostly taken for granted that any proof of the effect of reading is some evidence of the proof of the effectiveness of the library system. It is possible to offer more direct proof.

There is first the historical proof of the growth of the system, and, as a general rule, systems which grow are successful ones. Growth may be a sign of success in a system but this may have a bad effect on another system if one system is parasitically growing upon the other, a cancer being the obvious example. As noted, other parasitical systems may be for the good, as with the gestation of a mammal. The library system appears to be more analogous to the second example if one views a recorded communication as being the birth of knowledge. However, it is equally possible to state that, just as a child may be imprinted with unfortunate hereditary attributes, so too may a book be badly influenced by the mind of its author. There is little debate about this. The controversy revolves around the proposition that a bad book harms its readers and the attendant difficulties of finding empirical proof. In any case, the argument mainly centers on emotional effects and pays no attention to the transmission of data and ideas. The list of influential books previously noted is proof of success in this area.

Apart from this generalized proof, there is the more specific proof in the form of comment about libraries from a wide variety of sources. All of the comments apparently assume that the system is effective; some of it is critical and cynical; most of it concerns the public library system;

and most of it is favorable. The following comments are highly selective:
From literature:

My library
was dukedom large enough. (Shakespeare)

Knowing I loved my books, he furnished me
From mine own library with volumes that
I prize above my dukedom. (Shakespeare)

Come and take choice of all my library
And so beguile thy sorrow. (Shakespeare)

Twenty-two acknowledged concubines and a library of 62,000
volumes attested to the variety of his inclinations; and from the
productions which he left behind him, it appears that the former
as well as the latter were designed for use as well as ostentation.
(Gibbon)

A man will turn over half a library to make one book. (Johnson)

In each of these quotations, the value of libraries is acknowledged as
being worthwhile, but others are more condemning.

No place affords a more striking conviction of the vanity of
human hope than a public library. (Johnson)

Another agency for the radiation of light in the average town
first mentioned is the Municipal Free Library . . . . The chief
result of the penny-in-the-pound rate is to supply women, old
and young with outmoded, viciously respectable, viciously
sentimental fiction. . . . No Municipal Library can hope to be
nearer than 25 years to date. . . . That youthful miss in torpidity
over that palimpsest of filth is what the Free Library has to show
as the justification of its existence. I know what I am talking
about.   (Bennett).

The latter view was taken by many of the opposers of the free public library movement, but such opposition was eventually defeated. Ernest Savage claims that his father expressed a similar view when asked what a public library was:

> A place where people go to get books for nothing—just nothing, at the ratepayer's expense. And newspapers too. Making all people think alike, with their rubbish.[1]

A different approach was taken by Casanova, who became a librarian late in life and comments as follows on the research value of libraries and on access to them:

> Two or three weeks after my arrival the Prince of Santa Croce heard me complaining of the obstacles to research in Roman Libraries and he offered to give me an introduction to the Superior of the Jesuits. I accepted the offer, and was made free of the library. I could not only go and read when I liked but I could, on writing my name down, take books away with me. The Keepers of the library always brought me candles when it grew dark, and their politeness was so great that they gave me the key to a side door, so that I could slip in and out as I pleased.[2]

The educational value of libraries is referred to by Edward Edwards in his evidence to the Select Committee of 1849:

> I believe that the want of accessibility of good books is one case of the backwardness of this country in respect to education among large portions of the populations.[3]

One nonlibrarian and social historian thought that public libraries were successful as an educational force:

> Run as a public utility, the public libraries have never tried to impose their will upon either their customers or their suppliers. Tacitly excluding trash they have taken their part in the educational system very seriously, in providing for special needs such as a children's department and reference department, in assis-

ting the student through the publication of select lists on a variety of topics, and generally striking a happy balance between the demands of the low-brow and high-brow sections of the reading world.[4]

It is a happy balance which led other commentators to claim that the public library has a middle-class image. Thus the Richard Hoggart statement, "The public library has no appeal," when speaking of working-class reading habits.

As might be imagined, official statements on the effect of libraries are often much more cautious and circumspect: "We are conscious that now is not the best time to recommend that more resources be put into a particular service and especially into one where direct benefits to the community cannot easily be demonstrated."[5]

This was the official statement of a working committee of the Scottish Education Department which was to devise standards for the public library service. It is reasonable to ask why standards were produced at all when the working committee seemed so unsure that any benefit was to be derived. It can only be assumed that such a statement derived from the committee's desire to have facts and opinions substantiated by empirical research, but that, in their heart of hearts, the members knew that there were benefits. It can be presumed that they thought that they were valuable ones since the standards produced, if implemented, would entail a considerable increase in the expenditure on public libraries.

A similar cautionary statement was made in a similar report on public libraries in England and Wales: "The assessment of the efficiency of a library is a complicated task involving consideration of many factors in the light of varied local circumstances."[6]

Allowing the fact it is a complicated task, it could be claimed that the "consideration of many factors" has taken place throughout history on a global scale and under every possible local circumstance.

Indeed, almost every survey of libraries which has questioned people on what they think of library services has shown that there may be many specific complaints, but, in general terms, the majority of people are satisfied. The conclusions of one survey puts it thus: "The evidence suggests that the [public] libraries do not present a major target for criticism at least in the view of the public in the areas surveyed."[7]

Some librarians are concerned about this kind of evidence, claiming that the public is conditioned to a poor service and that any general sample of it must show satisfaction. It is pointed out that the specific complaints are sufficient in themselves to warrant attention, and their cause may generate considerable frustration to individual users. Librarianship is, finally, a service to individuals and there is no room for complacency if even a small minority of readers remain unsatisfied. It is often claimed that more specific surveys should be done with people who make an intensive rather than a casual use of libraries; the detailed faults in the system would then be more fully recorded.

An attempt to gauge the effectiveness of the intensive use of a library was undertaken by the British National Reference Library of Science and Invention in 1970.[8]

On six days over a period of three weeks, 3,065 reader visits to the library were sampled by means of a questionnaire to the reader on each visit. In overall terms, a clear majority of 74 percent got satisfaction from the visit, 16 percent were partly satisfied, and 5 percent unsatisfied. Even in more specific terms, the satisfaction rate was high. In searching "patent formalities," 82 percent were satisfied. The lowest satisfaction rate —74 percent—was reached by those engaged in "education or study" in the library. There were some interesting statistics on the casual retrieval of information: 14 percent claimed that they found useful information on their specific requests from unexpected sources, and some 20 percent that they had found useful information other than that for which they had specifically come.[9] It is clear that the majority of readers found the library useful and effective.

Further evidence of the effect of libraries is to be found in the more spontaneous comments of individual users, and it could be claimed that if the service is finally for individuals, then this type of comment is excellent evidence.

For instance, the cyclic nature of the library system is often shown by autobiographical comments of authors and writers. The following example consists of excerpts from the autobiography of Johnny Speight who, although he has not written much, has created, in Alf Garnett and his American counterpart, Archie Bunker, one of the great comic-satirical imaginative characters of all time, a character created very much from Speight's physical and reading environment:

> Bernard Shaw was alive in those days and I was always reading
> some remark of his in the newspapers. They were always very
> funny and I imagined him a stand-up comic like Tommy Trinder,

and I thought I must catch his act one day. Then, looking in
Canning Town Public Library for something to read, I saw this
shelf of books and I thought: "Christ. He writes as well." The
first book of his I read was "Immaturity", a novel. Reading Shaw
was to me at that time, I suppose, as near as one could get to a
kind of divine revelation. It was as though a light had been turned on and every dark recess lit by sweet reason; or like coming
up against cool clear sanity in a madhouse and the whole of life
was made to look brighter, and more hopeful than ever before.

Since reading Shaw I have come into contact with other great
writers, dramatists, philosophers, economists, thinkers, poets
and advocates, and hawkers of all manner of philosophies and
ways of life, but none has influenced me more, or made the
same impact on my mind that Shaw did. If God could write he
couldn't write better than Shaw. The mystery of life is a mystery
to all of us but the lunacies it is prone to are shown nowhere
better than in the works of Shaw.[10]

Well, Peter and I at about this time were getting hooked on
Steinbeck and Marx and Engels (this was just before Shaw).
Ivy thought they were a chain store. And the tramp was
our tame Steinbeck character. Steinbeck was the first
good novelist I'd read. Up until then all I'd read was
fiction and all the characters in these books were imaginery
and only lived in the minds of their authors, they were stillborn on to the page and their feelings were about as human
as the paper they were written on.

Steinbeck, on the other hand, was writing about people who
lived in the world as I knew it, and not just in his own mind.
This kind of writing was a revelation to Peter and I and we
went around Clacton discovering Steinbeck characters every-
where. The whole of Clacton was Steinbeck. The tramp was
Steinbeck, Ivy was Steinbeck. Some people, like the custom-
ers in this awful Guest House, weren't Steinbeck because they
weren't real.

I found writers of characters like this much more interesting.
Well, they were writing about people like myself, people up
against this business of trying to live without being exploited
too much by the other bastards.[11]

The satirical nature of the Garnett political caricature shows the influence of Shavian philosophy, and the basic humanity of his character reflects the depiction of a Steinbeck character.

One further and final method of showing how the use of library stock
has helped writers is to note the acknowledgments paid to them in authors'
prefaces and introductions.

If any sample of books is chosen, not at random but from the point of
view that the subject is one which is likely to have needed book research,
it is more than likely that over 50 percent of the authors will have paid
tribute to the help of libraries and librarians. To quote only one example:
"To the librarians, particularly those at Cornell University, the Library of
Congress, University of Virginia, and University of N. Carolina who have
aided in the location of needed materials. . . . " This is from E. D. Johnson's
History of Libraries in the Western World, a book which, in its turn, has
been borrowed from a library and used as a source of evidential data for
this work—a simple example of the cyclic system of man's mind → creation
→ manuscript → book → library → another mind → a different creation →
manuscript, and so on.

The fact that there is a different creation is the effect. The strength of
the effect must be left to the critics, to the individuals who read the new
creation, and, perhaps most of all, to history.

NOTES

1. Savage, E. A., *A Librarian's Memories* (Grafton, 1952), p. 9.
2. Powell, L. C., *Books in My Baggage* (Constable, 1960), p. 31.
3. Great Britain, House of Commons, Sessional Papers. *Report from the Select
   Committee on Public Libraries, Together with the Proceedings of the Committee*
   (Her Majesty's Stationery Office, 1849), pp. 20-21.
4. Steinberg, S. G., *Five Hundred Years of Printing* (Penguin, 1955), p. 231.
5. Scottish Education Department, *Standards for the Public Library Service in
   Scotland* (Her Majesty's Stationery Office, 1969), p. 5.
6. Great Britain, Department of Education and Science, *Standards of Public Library Service in England and Wales* (Her Majesty's Stationery Office, 1962),
   p. 44.

7. Luckham, B., *The Library in Society* (Library Association, 1971), p. 90.
8. Sandison, A., and Preskett, M., *Library Effectiveness Survey* (National Reference Library of Science and Invention, 1970).
9. Ibid., pp. 6-8.
10. Speight, J., *It Stands to Reason: A Kind of Autobiography* (M. Joseph, 1973), pp. 135-136.
11. Ibid., pp. 169-170.

Part Six

LIBRARIES PROMOTING COMMUNICATIONS

16
Publisher

By far the largest part of the output from the library system is the process of putting a reader in contact with the requisite work he has been seeking. This was theoretically postulated in Chapter 2 when the analysis of three communication systems in terms of their input, throughput, and output showed that allowing access to the memory store was the output from a library system. Subsequent chapters have provided evidence that in practice, throughout history, civilized man has actively involved himself in the growth and preservation of his memory bank and that he has also, despite occasional proof to the contrary, taken pains to ensure that easy access to the store is available to all users. Considerable effort has also been applied to the retrieval problem. Man has also philosophically concerned himself about the effects of the output.

One minor yet important type of output of the system occurs when the library user is offered a communication which has been created by the library itself as distinct from ones which have been created by other bodies and stored by the library. The library as a promoter of communications can be looked at in two ways: as a publisher, and as an agency for the organization of cultural activities.

As a publisher, the library has a fair record of achievement. In the beginning it was as much publisher as library. Attached as it was to the religious temple, it became part of a system which educated the chosen few in the twins of literacy, reading and writing, and having taught writing, it then retained the scribes to produce texts: "Every sanctuary possessed its library and school, 'The House of the Tablet' or 'The House of the Seal' in which temple archives and liturgical texts were preserved, and the young were instructed in the art of writing."[1]

The temple library of Assurbanipal apparently employed many scribes and scholars to edit and revise. In fact, many of the tablets in the library were copies of non-Assyrian texts. There was a school for scribes there as there was at Nippur. As with Babylonian libraries, the early archives and libraries of Egypt were under the direction of specially trained scribes, and it is possible that the wealthier collectors of private libraries may have employed scribes. It has also been claimed that the Dead Sea Scrolls of the Hebrew congregation of Essenes are a collection of master texts which were copied by scribes and sent to outlying communities.[2]

The Alexandrian Library also provides us with examples. One author remarks as follows: "These enormous labors of textual criticism and literary preservation and probably reconstruction of an entire literature, the greatest yet known, constitute our imperishable obligation to the Alexandrian Scholar Age."[3]

Indicative of the extent to which the Alexandrian Library was prepared to go was the practice of meeting ships entering the harbor to find out if they were carrying any literary works with them. If so, these works were confiscated and taken to the library, where a fair copy was made, this being given to the owner, the original being added to stock. These works were referred to as "books of the ships," and one could view them as an early form of legal deposit.[4] A variation of this practice was employed when official state "originals" of Aeschylus, Sophocles, and Euripides were borrowed from Athens. The originals were kept, and copies were made and sent to Athens. There was a forfeit in this instance: a deposit of fifteen talents was not returned because of the switch.[5]

Early Roman libraries were in temples and, like Egypt and Babylonia, there were schools for the priests. It would seem that many of the Roman writers had private libraries, Cicero (106-43 B.C.) being an outstanding example. One of his friends, Titus Pomponius Atticus, was a book collector with some 20,000 rolls. He was also a publisher; his slaves were taught to copy the works of popular authors and these copies were sold.[6] Sometimes more than 1,000 copies were produced.[7] The original could be dictated to a dozen or more scribes.[8]

The medieval monasteries which kept a spark of scholarship alive throughout the Dark Ages did not do so only by the maintenance of libraries but also by the establishment of *scriptoria* ("writing rooms"), for which it was necessary to train scribes: "[Cassiodorus (485-574 A.D.)] established the first mediaeval scriptorium and the principles and prac-

tices of library management which endured until the invention of printing."
Cassiodorus was a Roman nobleman who, after the siege of Rome in
546 A.D., had destroyed the Palatine and Ulpian libraries, conceived the
idea of establishing a Christian university like the Alexandrian. His monastery was established in Calabria and named "Vivarium."

The scriptorium and the library seem to have almost always been in the
same room, and their separation to allow for the expanding book stocks
with a specially equipped library room was a gradual process. In passing,
it might be noticed that not all scribes were in love with their work; some
unwilling ones had their wine withheld as punishment, another had to be
bound by fetters to keep him at his work, and an Irish scribe, with typical humor, glossed a Latin text with "St. Patrick of Armagh, deliver me
from writing."[9]

The essential nature of monastic organization ensured that libraries
were very closely connected with the production of books. The impact
of the invention of moveable type saw to it that there was never such a
close connection again.

Commenting previously on the invention of moveable print, it was
noted that it was a fine example of necessity being the mother of invention.
It might have been expected that the work needed for the creation of the printing press took place in the monasteries, but the fact is that there was a steady
decline in the scriptoria throughout the fourteeth century, partly due to
the spread of education, which created a demand for textbooks which
would not be supplied by the monasteries, and partly because of increasing wealth outside the monasteries.[10] The shift from monastic to secular
publishing had already commenced when Gutenberg applied himself to
the problem of "regimenting" his "soldiers of lead." His achievement, as
we have seen, created a tool, the use of which was to spread throughout
the world and give such an impetus to the spread and need for knowledge
that the art could not be contained within the monasteries.

Very few monasteries seem to have established presses. Two which did,
however, were the Benedictine Abbey of Subiaco near Rome and the Abbey
of SS. Ulric and Afra of Augsburg, both of which had excellent scriptoria.
The Subiaco Abbey housed the first press in Italy, although it was manned
by two Germans who brought the craft from Germany. They stayed for only
a short time and then moved to Rome. The press at the Augsburg abbey
was the first in that town.[11]

If a publisher is defined as a person or group of persons who gives the

necessary financial capital for the production of a book, then publishers
existed from the beginnings of moveable print. Indeed, much of the evidence we have to connect Gutenberg with the invention comes from law
suits connected with loans of money which he had negotiated and then
found difficulty in paying back. Inevitably, as the trade grew, more and
more specialization was introduced in the nature of division of work. One
development was the emergence of a publisher who financially controlled
the production of a work, making payments to and therefore, in a sense,
employing author, printer, binder, and bookseller. This took place mainly
in the seventeenth century, one source claiming that Humphrey Moseley,
publisher of Milton in the 1640s, was the first in England, although another
points out that by the end of the seventeenth century, imprints were still
phrased, "Printed by Thos. Cotes, for Andrew Crook, and are to be sold at
the Black Bare in Paul's Church-yard," thus still giving prominence to both
printer and bookseller.[12] The gradual change of imprints to display the
publisher's name indicates his rise to power. The library's part of the division of labor was that it became the store for the end product of the trade,
with only occasional ventures into the author-printer-publisher areas of
work. By the time libraries were of any size, the printing trade was well-
established, and there are few, if any, examples of early libraries which
owned printing presses for the express purpose of printing items for sale
or distribution, although some may have been retained as museum pieces.
In the twentieth century the printing process has become so much more
complex and expensive that new technologies of duplicating, "near-print"
methods, have been evolved so that costs can be reduced. These methods
have been used by libraries for many of their publications so that libraries
have become printers as well as authors and publishers. The examples of
early university presses are misleading. These presses were established by
the university authorities rather than the library authorities, although no
doubt many librarians were marginally involved. They are better viewed as
examples of secular education in the form of universities taking their communication responsibilities seriously. Two professors at the Sorbonne in
Paris were responsible for inviting the first printers, three Germans, to
France where they set up the press within the university.

By far the greatest contribution to publishing that libraries have made
has been in coping with problems of bibliographical control by the production of printed catalogues and booklists. This was a natural development
since they were most directly involved with the problem. The outline of

the quantitative growth of libraries in Chapter 4 shows the enormous nature of the problem, and Chapter 12, on the retrieval problem, notes the difficulties libraries have always had in making records of their stocks. Despite these difficulties, it was stated that countless numbers of library users had gained access to library stocks via catalogues. The published printed catalogues of libraries have not only allowed the users of a specific library to own a catalogue of its stock but have allowed other libraries and other library users to purchase them and thus build up a valuable collection of bibliographical tools, helping them to identify and trace works which they do not stock and to locate for possible interloan.

A recent work by Robert Collison is devoted entirely to the published catalogues of libraries in the English-speaking world. In an enumeration, he lists over 600 works, which do not seem all too many, considering the possible numbers which might have been published.[13] Collison in no way claims to be definitive and has obviously selected the more important publications from the more important libraries. He lists only two from the John Rylands Library, whereas another source notes five such publications.[14] Despite his selectivity and the obvious omission of many minor booklists, the small number reminds us of the practical problems of producing catalogues. The difficulty is also shown by the lack of general catalogues which attempt to cover all stock. Useful as those which have been published have been, it is often the more specialized catalogues of particular areas of stock which have proved most useful to the researcher.

The following examples of types of published catalogues have been culled from the above two sources.

Of the general catalogues, the most important are obviously those of the great national libraries with legal-deposit collections. Any general catalogue of theirs acts as a basic national bibliography, collecting the vast bulk of a nation's book output in one work. The three supreme examples are the catalogues of the British Museum (BM), the U.S. Library of Congress (LC), and the French Bibliothèque Nationale (BN).

Of these, the most fully developed is that of the LC. Since 1956, its supplements have been published as the *National Union Catalogue* because from that date it included not only its own stock but entries and locations for important foreign works in North American research libraries. The success of this venture is such that a retrospective cumulative catalogue is planned; its completion date is expected to be 1980. Entitled *The National Union Catalogue, Pre-1956 Imprints,* it will consist of 610 volumes with an estimated 13 million entries and will locate items in some 2,000 American and Canadian libraries. The venture led Collison to comment, "The early dream of Paul Otlet (1868-1945) of establishing a complete record of the world's bibliographical output is in fact nearing realisation."[15]

True!—if he had added, after "output," "of works of importance to research workers."

The BM *General Catalogue of Printed Books* included works added to stock up to 1955, but it has been updated by a decennial supplement covering 1956-1965. The BN *Catalogue général des livres imprimés,* begun in 1897, is still in process, having reached the letter "W" by 1975. It has failed to make use of the modern printing processes which have speeded the production of the other two.

Other types of libraries have produced general catalogues, but most have been unable to keep up-to-date. There is one example of almost 100 years being taken to complete six volumes— the *Bibliothecae Chethamensis Catalogus* (1791-1883). Endowed in the town of Manchester in 1653 by Humphrey Chetham, Chetham's Library is still operational and open to the public.

As for universities, Oxford has the honor of having published the first printed catalogue of any European library— the *Catalogus Librorum Bibliothecae Publicae Quam . . . T. Bodleius . . . in Academia Oxoniensis Nuper Instituit* (1605). Further general catalogues were produced, but the final attempt was in 1843 when a three-volume work was produced. Cambridge never attempted a general catalogue.

There are few twentieth-century general printed catalogues by universities, although between 1918 and 1923 Edinburgh did produce the three-volume *Catalogue of the Printed Books in the Library,* a work which is still in print.

There is some possibility that the new technologies being applied to cataloguing procedures may encourage libraries with important collections to produce printed catalogues. As recently as 1963, two of the campuses of the University of California produced printed catalogues: Berkeley a 115-volume *Author-Title Catalogue,* and Los Angeles a 129-volume *Dictionary Catalogue.* Five-yearly cumulations to both are promised. The works are produced by the firm of G. K. Hall, which has used the photo-lithographic technique of copying the card-catalogue entries and printing them in a reduced size. The alternative prospect is that with the MARC methods,it is in the future going to be relatively easy to produce cumulated and up-to-date catalogues from computer output.

Of the 600 works listed by Collison, the vast majority are of a special-ized nature, and it is here that many more libraries can aid in solving the problem of bibliographical control by publishing select catalogues of their specialized collections. The large national libraries still contribute in the specialized fields: in Collison's list, forty-nine published catalogues are credited to the British Museum and thirty-three to the Library of Congress. There is naturally a concentration on material which is either unique or scarce.

Just as it was difficult to select appropriate and indicative examples of influential books in Chapter 13, it is more so to show by examples the wide and varied range of printed catalogues which have been published by libraries to make known their holdings in specialized areas. The good habit of libraries making special collections in particular spheres is a fur-ther example of the emphasis on the memory part of the system. The published catalogue is the publicity man thinks it deserves.

Librarians who read this work will have no difficulty in remembering examples and others will have no difficulty in finding them. Enter any library of any reasonable size and you will find such catalogues in their collection of bibliographies, either publications of their own or of other libraries.

Smaller libraries which cannot or need not produce full or specialized catalogues still produce booklists to help readers gain knowledge of stock. Simplified duplicating, or near-print, methods of production make this economically possible. Innumerable lists have been produced by all types of library. Their range of coverage is wide. There are accessions lists of new works from academic, scholarly, and special libraries for readers who wish to keep a constant check on new stock. From public libraries, less formal lists are compiled on popular subjects, individual authors, hobbies, and topical and seasonal events. Special libraries make exhaustive and analytical lists for narrow subject fields of direct interest to their readers. The range of possibilities is limitless and leaves considerable scope for li-brarians to exercise their imaginations in listing and presenting stock in a less rigid way than their formal classifications do.

Booklists comprise the bulk of library publications, but there are a few contributions in other areas.

An annual report is commonly compiled, especially by public libraries. It is often a formal report of a librarian to a committee and may be printed for prestige value. It provides an opportunity for a librarian to review his year's work and, as a separate exercise, to consider the future. It is of little value to the majority of readers, but its value to the profession can be considerable. As a source of data concerning a particular library and as a source of trends over a number of libraries, it is invaluable.

The publication of periodicals of scholarly interest is now uncommon, and the few which do appear are from large libraries with research interests.

Of all library publications, the great printed catalogues remain the most prestigious even though little cost/benefit analysis has been done on their effects—or the effects of any other library publication for that matter. On the one hand, there is the prima facie case that because they are published and people do receive them, effect takes place; on the other hand, it is held that publication is a matter of professional prestige and pride.

Clearly, the modern library has specialized in publications germane to its own work and has seldom entered into competition with the commercial book trade. As a promoter of cultural activities, it has in some ways either competed with or complemented other communication agencies. This is a topic which is worthy of separate treatment in the next chapter.

NOTES

1. Thompson, J. W., *Ancient Libraries* (Archon Books, 1962), p. 1.
2. Johnson, E. D., *History of Libraries in the Western World,* 2nd ed. (Scarecrow Press, 1970), pp. 24, 27, 35, 38.
3. Parsons, E. A. *The Alexandrian Library: The Glory of the Hellenic World* (American Elsevier Publishing Co.), p. 220.
4. Ibid., pp. 163-164.
5. Thompson, *Ancient Libraries,* p. 23.
6. Johnson, *History of Libraries in the Western World,* pp. 72-77.
7. Savage, E. A., *The Story of Libraries and Book Collecting* (Routledge, 1908), p. 31.
8. Thompson, *Ancient Libraries,* p. 91.
9. Thompson, J. W., *The Medieval Library* (Hafner, 1967), pp. 36, 37, 601.
10. Ibid., p. 612.
11. Steinberg, S. H., *Five Hundred Years of Printing* (Penguin, 1955), pp. 40, 142.
12. Esdaile, A., *Student's Manual of Bibliography* (Allen & Unwin, 1954), pp. 134-135; Steinberg, S. H., *Five Hundred Years of Printing* (Penguin, 1955), pp. 91-93.
13. Collison, R., *Published Library Catalogues* (Mansell, 1973), pp. 107-169.
14. Burton, M., *Famous Libraries of the World* (Grafton, 1937), passim.

17

Organizer of Cultural Activities

In the brief examination of some of the theories of general systems in Chapter 1, Law 6 was stated as follows: "The dynamic relationship between individuals is either (a) parasitic, (b) competitive, or (c) complementary."

In relating this law to a library system, it was noted that there were parasitic relationships between society and its libraries which were of a cyclic nature. Of the three elements, however, it was postulated that the concept of a library as a complementary system to man's communication system was the most important. The subsequent chapters have, it is believed, sustained this view, as they also sustain the view that there is little evidence that they have been highly effective in competing against the aberrations of the human system.

It was suggested at that point that the concept of the library system as a competitor was best shown by relating libraries to other communication systems developed by man subsequent to his development of libraries. It is true that other systems may not have been produced with the concept of competition in mind and that in the long term they must be seen as complementary. However, in the short term, the very fact that the systems are basically the same in that they are outputting information, yet different in that they use different media and formats, effectively means that they can be seen to be in a state of competition. The concept is valid in that any competitor is forced to examine his own resources in terms of strengths and weaknesses so that he may concentrate on the strengths and attempt to reinforce the weaknesses if he can. In many instances, it is impossible to improve weaknesses to any great competitive degree and this forces greater concentration on the strengths, a fact which makes the system complementary rather than competitive. The relationships between

competing and complementary entities are subtle but are worthy of attention because, if they can clearly be identified, they have a strong bearing on
the orientation of the objectives of the library system. In attempting such
a clarification, it is necessary to identify the systems with which libraries
can be compared. Presented in a chronological order of historical development these are:

1. Man himself, and his other leisure and work activities
2. The commerical trade in recorded communications (the book trade,
   record trade, etc.)
3. Museums
4. The theatre
5. Education by formal institutions
6. Cinema
7. Broadcasting (radio, television)
8. Computers

The direct relationship between man and his libraries has already been
established. The library is his collective memory and in quantitative terms
is clearly supreme, but it may be less sure in its retrieval and will frequently
be slower. On its own, its creative ability is nil, but it complements man's
mind by feeding it some of the data on which the re-creation of knowledge
is nourished. Data are also received from other sources. Information from
a library is at best second-hand and is not comprehensible to a person without a knowledge of the real world as a referral point; in this sense, second-
hand information only adds to real information as it has been directly perceived. The remarkable ability of man to think in terms of abstractions is,
after all, only a method of speeding the thought process since all abstractions can be seen as symbols of reality, the symbols being more convenient to thought than reality itself. Much second-hand information comes
to a person by word of mouth, and it has to be conceded that more information is received from this source than from any other. In modern
times, we include broadcasting media as aural sources, but despite their
addition, much information is received by man during his leisure and work
activities. Indeed, it seems that it could well have been the communicatory
needs of work or leisure which established the necessity of speech. While,
on the one hand, oral communication is immediate and capable of conveying more emotion than the printed word, from a rational point of

view it is all the more suspect as a means of conveying hard knowledge
or fact. To offer two extreme examples: the words of poetry often lie
dormant on a page of print and only come to life if spoken with the neces-
ary inflections, rhythms, and intensities which are its essence; on the other
hand, the facts recorded in a reference work are much more reliably stored
and transmitted by the printed word than by word of mouth. For the quick
transmission of news and for emotional intensity, the spoken word remains
supreme. The library cannot compete in speed as an agency for the transmission of news, but by means of modern audio and visual media it can
stimulate the living quality of the spoken word. In some instances, it
has competed with the second-hand nature of the mass media by promoting live performances. The wide extent of story hours for children has
given an opportunity for the continuation of one of the earliest uses to
which man put speech, and the empathy which can be created between
the teller and the listeners, to the mutual advantage of both in heighten-
ing the effect of the message, still cannot be equaled by the second-hand
media.

Many libraries have also promoted lecture series which can be compared to those initiated by educational institutions. Historically, the two
have always existed side by side, and it is only the modern era of specialization which has apparently separated them. The close connection between libraries, the art of writing, and the arts of teaching and learning
has already been noted to have existed in the temples of the early civilizations of man. The Greek word "museum," meaning "temple of the
Muses," was also used to describe a meeting place for scholars to communicate both by word of mouth and by the written word. (The Muses
were the patron goddesses of art and literature.) The situation at Alexandria is the most outstanding example. The connection has been described
as follows: "Here was to arise the Alexandrian, handmaid to the Museum,
indeed its natural complement."[1] The influence that this "University of
Egypt" had on cultural civilization is incalculable. During the Middle
Ages, when teaching and learning were largely confined to monasteries,
there was a close connection between library and monastery, and when
the Renaissance gave the impetus to lay institutions, they too had to supply themselves with libraries. The public library, intended for every man,
was well established before compulsory education, and the tax-supported
ones, which in their early days were modeled on the Mechanics Institute
movement, often promoted educational communications. The Manchester

library was offering lectures as early as 1852, and the library in Liverpool, not to be outdone, began extensive lecture programs from 1865 onward, accumulating annual attendances of almost 200,000.[2] The tradition has continued in spite of increased competition from the media, although, if large audiences are to be attracted, it becomes more and more necessary to have a "personality" lecturer, the charisma often attained via another medium. The conclusion to be drawn is that a small but discriminating audience is still prepared to take the time to attend live performances. An example of a modern series is that offered by the Glasgow Public Libraries; their winter series of six lectures in 1970-1971 was attended by a record 2,540,[3] only one-tenth of the Liverpool figure of 100 years ago.

When lecture programs by modern libraries are put into the total perspective of programs given by educational institutions and the mass media, it can be held that it is only tradition which keeps them going, their mass influence being negligible.

Specialization has also brought about some separation of museum and library. The museum has become an institution for the display of three-dimensional communications, with the further specialization of the art gallery. There are still strong connections between all three. Their basic communicatory function is undeniable; museums and art galleries frequently have collections of books to help their staffs in their work, and libraries not infrequently have paintings and prints as part of their stocks and, occasionally, three-dimensional items. At the local level, the first tax-supported libraries in the United Kingdom (at Canterbury, Salford, and Warrington) were established under the Museums Act of 1845, and such acts have existed for both libraries and museums since 1919. It has, however, become more and more necessary for their staffs to specialize in their own areas, despite the fact the same committee administers to both.[4] A subtle change in the importance placed on each institution by society is highlighted by these words: "When once the library (or the art gallery or museum) were the great symbols of civic pride, responsibility and public support to the worthy, to-day cities compete to be the sites of universities."[5]

What has happened, of course, is that libraries have become commonplace, whereas the number of universities remains limited and this creates competition for them.

The difficulty of separating the complementary from the competitive nature of libraries is encountered when they are related to the trades which commercially sell the products which libraries stock.

Prior to moveable print, stock in libraries was mainly unique, but with mass production of books, the trade could claim, and did, that library copies used by readers effectively reduced the number of copies sold and therefore affected the economy of the trade. Libraries, on their part, argued that they helped the trade by buying copies, that this especially helped new authors, and that they helped to advertise the books they bought, thus creating a further demand. What is certain is that both systems have been growing in terms of demand, and it seems as though, in the long term, they combine to form a cyclic system with more benefit than detriment to each other. The twentieth-century paperback revolution eased the situation. The movement in the United Kingdom started in 1935 with Allen Lane's *Penguin Books,* which heralded a series of paperback lists in which birds were used as the publisher's device to symbolize the great venture of bringing culture in book form to a mass reading population at prices it could afford. In passing, it should be noted that high typographical standards were maintained, although cheap paper was often used to reduce costs. Most other large publishers followed suit, and it is not uncommon to find bookshops entirely devoted to the sale of paperbacks (sometimes solely Penguins, as one of Foyle's in London). Liraries have usually bought hardbacks, and they claim that there must have been many occasions when, having read a hardback edition in the library, a reader has bought the paperback edition of the same book and perhaps other books by the same author.

In general, libraries and the trade have had good relations apart from a few skirmishes. The trade takes exception to its paperbacks being bound by libraries but can legally do nothing to stop this, except make it a condition of sale that it shall not be done "by way of trade" without prior permission of the publisher. In recent years it has also, especially via the Society of Authors, mounted a strong campaign for a "public lending right" to be established. By analogy with the public performing right, the claim is that the author and publisher should be reimbursed by a library every time a book is loaned. At this time, the matter lies unresolved, libraries being very concerned with the practical implications of the scheme. Many debaters concede that the principle is correct but argue that the practical difficulties are too great for the relatively small return to be gained. The best-selling author who is already well-rewarded financially tends to gain more, no matter what scheme is devised. Publishers and authors in the United Kingdom are already given protection by society in that the Restrictive Trades Practice Court in 1962 came to the conclusion that it was in the best interests of the public and the trade if the practice of not allowing booksellers to cut the publisher's price of a book continued. This affords the trade protection from possible price-cutting wars, a situation all too possible in modern commerce, particularly in the paperback market. This kind of competition between the systems is to be regretted. It is suggested that it is only of short-term significance; in the long term, the systems are much more complementary than competitive.

One further example might help to reinforce this point. On the occasions when libraries become publishers, thus placing themselves in direct competition with the trade, they seldom publish the kind of material which the trade is interested in. Obvious examples are catalogues, which are often subsidized in cost. As noted in the previous chapter, cheaper photolithographic methods of producing catalogues by photographing card catalogues have made this a more valid publishing.process. The firm of G.K. Hall of Boston, Massachusetts, has commercially produced numerous catalogues in this fashion. Here, the trade is taking advantage of the work of the library. Even when the professional associations of librarians enter the publishing field, it is to publish material directly associated with librarianship or bibliographical tools which most publishers would consider noncommercial. The *British Humanities Index* and the *British Technology Index* are examples of good indices to periodical literature published by the British Library Association. The American Library Association's publication of *Guide to Reference Books,* a work now in its eighth edition, is an excellent example of what has become a standard work. Libraries sometimes act as trial markets for publishers in gauging a revival in demand for a book which is out of print.

A comparison of the two systems reveals that they both disseminate books to readers, the basic difference being that the trade inevitably is motivated by monetary profit while the library is motivated by the needs of its readers. This means that the trade must deal with the wants of the masses and it is therefore oriented toward the best seller and deals with this remarkably well. It is to its credit, however, that it does make considerable attempts to deliver a work at an individual's request, but in this respect it is not so successful as the library interloan system. In the first place, the trade is mainly interested in books in print, although second-hand request systems do exist in the antiquarian market; in the second, while the publisher is only too willing to sell his product, the bookseller is put to a considerable amount of trouble with one-copy orders, and a satisfactory solution to the problem has still to be found if the letters airing grievances in book-trade journals are evidence. A statistical comparison of the resources of the two systems in the United Kingdom shows that the book trade has at its disposal some 240,000 titles in print, of which some 34,500 are paperbacks.[6] A quarter of a million is small compared with a probable 6 million in the library store.

The library system has extensive and, in the main, effective interloan systems, designed, altruistically and idealistically, to tap the total resources and make sure that no serious request by a reader is unsatisfied. The view can be taken that it is organized not only to overcome the deficiencies of individual library stocks but also the inadequacies of the book trade.

The theatre as a communication system can alsó be subjected to comparison with the library system. Basically, it is a system which man has created to allow himself the excitement, entertainment, and instruction of simulating his real-life patterns. No doubt there are good psychological explanations of why he has done this, but we need only accept the fact that he has and, from anthropological evidence, that he has from very early days. The theatre could be viewed as an extension of the story in that the plot, as well as being told, is enacted, which adds communicatory information and heightens the dramatic, comic, or descriptive effect. As early as 500 B.C., the Greeks built an open-air theatre in Athens to seat some 20,000 persons, a pattern which was frequently repeated in the Greco-Roman world. European theatres of the sixteenth century were enclosed and had much smaller audiences. The famous Globe of Elizabethan times had a capacity of 1,200. The electronic media of cinema, radio, and television are now capable of reaching audiences of millions simultaneously. To many people, the highlights of television programs are the productions of plays and repeats of previous film productions for the cinema. Dramatic productions are an integral part of society.

When a production is recorded in book or electronic form, it will find a place in the library store, as will the archive of the playwright's manuscript, the more so nowadays because of errors of the past which resulted in tremendous gaps in the library store, such as the lack of a single Shakespearean manuscript. Apart from complementing the theatre by storing its records, libraries have also helped by providing accommodation and sometimes financial resources to stage productions. Overall, this is complementing the theatre; any competition is only with the commercial side of the stage.

Many public library authorities which have lecture halls will occasionally allow the use of them for play productions, but this type of accommodation falls short of a true theatre with the necessary stage, lighting, and other props (an expensive additon within the budgets of only a few libraries). On the one hand, library authorities will allow the use of library space to amateur companies, thus considerably relieving their financial commitments, but some will also provide professional productions by using repertory companies, either resident or borrowed. It is seldom that the productions will fall to the level of a farce; a more varied program of classics, modern successes, tragedies, and comedies is likely to be offered in the best traditions of the repertory movement. The impact of television has seen a dramatic reduction in the number of commercial theatres, especially in the provinces. The promotion of theatre productions by libraries is clearly complementary and counterbalances this loss.

The cinema was the first electronic extension of the theatre. Its particular validity was that the capturing of a play on a recording medium allowed it to be replayed to ever-increasing audiences. The various technological achievements which made this possible are well represented in the list of influential books in *Printing and the Mind of Man.* [7] Although the technological groundwork was laid in the nineteenth century, it is the twentieth century which has seen its application to a mass medium. It is estimated that by 1970 there were 248,000 commercial fixed cinemas, providing 78 million seats throughout the world (excluding China). Some annual attendance figures of the same period are 920 million in the United States, 4,656 million in the USSR, and 176 million in the United Kingdom, thus representing annual attendances per person as 5, 19, and 3.2, respectively. [8] A quick comparison shows that inhabitants in the United Kingdom visit public libraries more often than the cinema. One estimate shows that the average interval between visits for members was twelve days, so that if we assume a membership of 25 percent of the population this would give forty-eight days, or seven times per year per person, a figure equal to twice the cinema attendances. [9] It should be remembered, however, that by 1970 the competition from television had considerably reduced cinema attendances. It could be speculatively suggested that the reason for high cinema attendances in Russia is due to factors such as illiteracy, fewer libraries, and limited television coverage. There are only two and a half times the number of television receivers in the USSR compared with the United Kingdom despite a population factor of four times.[10] Many librarians prophesied in the early days of cinema, and later radio and television, that the competition from these media would reduce the use of libraries. There were short recessions, but overall there has been an increase in library use, due no doubt to many factors. There has been some evidence of spin-off from the other media. A survey in 1967 showed some correlation between education broadcasts and subsequent borrowing on their topics from public libraries.[11] There are many examples of increased demand in libraries from the stimulation of other media. The most obvious, yet the one most often forgotten, is the demand in libraries of educational institutions, the most often quoted being the lengthening reservation lists for certain novels which have been re-created for cinema or television. There is also the reaction of "I've read the book, I must see the film," and the evidence of this is the film producer's search for plots from novels in preference to the creation of original stories and scripts. In additon to this spin-off from one medium to another, the library also complements the cinema by promoting the showing of films. This is a simple extension of a theatre production, and in one sense the word "simple" is appropriate, the showing of films being much more easily organized than a play. With modern advances in hardware and software, we now have inflammable film in cassettes for ease of use and reduction of damage, and self-feeding and rewinding projectors which are also easily transportable. Any reasonable lecture-theatre capable of blackout can quickly have a portable screen erected, and the system is operational. While the cost of prerecorded film is high, a large number are available for rent at rates which make showings to audiences as small as twenty feasible. As with the theatre, libraries have tended to be complementary to the film industry by filling a gap which it is unwilling, for harsh commercial reasons, to fill. The tendency is to show films which would have a very limited commercial viewing or those which may have had a good commercial success but are worth repeating to a limited but discriminating audience. There is often a strong cultural and educational value. In no way is this direct competition with the commercial cinema; it complements it by giving an opportunity to see films otherwise not available. Other organizations, such as educational institutions or film societies, play a similar role in promoting showings of non-commercial films, and it is possible that the library will cooperate in some way with them.

Even before its most popular period, the 1930s to the 1950s, the cinema was already being challenged by the second wonder of the electronic world—broadcasting.

Electronically, broadcasting is an extension of telegraphy, which is capable of sending a message from one point to another by means of a wire. Wireless telegraphy is capable of sending the message simultaneously to a number of different points where radios receive the signals. Broadcasting is the mass-medium application of this technique. In the United Kingdom, the first license for public broadcasting was given in 1922. The public corporation of the BBC was formed in 1927, and it remained in sole control until 1955 when the Independent Television Authority (ITA) was formed as a second corporation. While the other media of communication—libraries, the book trade, the press, theatre, and cinema—were reaching large audiences, they were not doing so simultaneously, and this factor made broadcasting the most important medium for news. At the present time, the 8 A.M. news on Radio 4 attracts 4 million listeners, which is far from being the largest audience but is a very substantial one. However, it could be pointed out that some 25 million copies (one for every two of population) of daily newspapers are published every day, which gives a larger potential of readers and possibly simultaneous reception. The largest number of listeners—11 million— is for "Family Favourites," a record-choice program, on Radio 2, Sundays at 12 noon; the lowest—50,000— for "Story Time" on Radio 4 and the plays on Radio 3.[12] An audience of 50,000 still far exceeds any attendance at the live theatre.

The large audience figures for radio broadcasting were exceeded with the introduction of television broadcasting. Begun in 1936, it was suspended during the war years and reintroduced in 1946. By 1952 only 14 percent of the population had television receivers, but by 1969 the percentage had risen to 94.2.

Television is the most advanced medium in mass communication. It adds a visual picture to a sound message and retains the advantage of simultaneous reception by delivering to the fireside at a remarkably low cost. It captures large audiences from the other media, particularly those which are similar. The drop in cinema audiences has already been referred to, and further statistics show the dramatic decline in Britain:[13]

Year	Total Cinema Attendances
1950	1,300,000,000
1970	200,000,000

In almost the same time span, radio listening was reduced by about 40 percent and television viewing increased by over 100 percent:[14]

Year (Oct/Dec)	Listening (per person)	Viewing (per person)
1952	14.55 hours per week	7.20 hours per week
1969	8.29 hours per week	16.20 hours per week

The effect on newspaper circulation was not so dramatic in total copies sold, but many newspapers have been forced to cease publication, the casualty rate being particularly high in local publications, although a number of nationals also suffered. A silver lining in this recession is a rise in the circulation of the higher-quality press, such as the London *Times.*[15] In the industry, the economic balance between production costs, revenue from circulation, and, more vitally, revenue from advertising continues to be knife-edged.

The effect on loans by public libraries is apparently negligible; they rose from 314 million in 1950-1951 to 445 million in 1958-1959.[16] The British Library Association ceased to collect statistics on loans after 1960-1961. The question of whether there would have been a greater increase but for the time demands of television must remain unanswered.

The concept of administering television by a public corporation free of direct government control has gained British broadcasting the reputation of being the best in the world. An analysis of its program content is as follows:[17]

Information	25.2 percent
Light Entertainment	22.9 percent
Education	20.5 percent
For Special Audiences	13.6 percent
Arts, Letters, Sciences	12.9 percent
Advertising	3.7 percent
For Ethnic Minorities	1.1 percent

The close balance of education, recreation, and information, those abstractions of effects of communications so beloved by librarians, is some evidence of a real attempt by the corporations to give fair shares to all audience demands. It is also often pointed out that attacks on program content come from so many different sects and pressure groups of opposite doctrines that they can only indicate the overall neutrality of the corporations. Be this as it may, the one glaring defect of the medium is that it is geared to produce for mass audiences and can offer little choice to discriminating viewers, with only three channels and no cable TV available at the moment. The present debate about the allocation of a fourth channel centers around the issue of whether it should be allocated as another for advertising, thus tending to bring program content to the lowest common denominator, or should be used to strengthen the educational aspects, which have been given an impetus with the Open University programs. Even if the decision is for educational expansion, it is expected that audiences will be numbered in tens, if not hundreds, of thousands.

The large audiences at the moment are for entertainment and certain newsreels.[18] The Sunday night film on BBC 1 attracts between 10 and 20 million. The serialization of the "Forsyte Saga" on Sunday evenings gained 15 million viewers and substantially reduced church attendances. In both these instances, it is interesting to note that the programs were originally produced for other media. "News at 10" of the IBA and the BBC's news at 9 P.M. both attract 9.5 million. Of the smaller audiences, an estimated 750,000 viewed "Chronicle" (a historical program) on BBC 2, and 250,000 addicts watched the jaded "Animal, Vegetable, Mineral" parlor game. Smaller audiences almost certainly exist for educational broadcasts. For instance, in 1971 the total number of students undertaking the Open University Foundation Course was 24,000, and programs were shown for specializing sections of this total.

Assuming that 25 percent of the population holds membership in public libraries and that the average frequency of visits is one every twelve days, it is possible that 1 million go to a public library every day. Allowing a generous 250,000 visits to other libraries, the total figure falls far short of television audiences. In this kind of quantitative analysis, the library is a poor second to television, but it is possible that the daily attendances do exceed those of the cinema.

This kind of quantitative comparison helps to sustain some of the differences between media, but also helps to hide the essential difference between libraries and all others. If libraries are considered a mass medium, it is only because those in the public sector are in theory attempting to find a 100 percent membership. They are not searching for the simultaneous mass audience of broadcasting and, at a different level, the cinema and the press. For the short-term dissemination of news information, ephemeral comment, and entertainment, the mass media are excellent, but it is the long-term storage of communications in libraries which makes them clearly the best medium for more leisurely, and thus more considered, study. They have a very vital part to play in complementing and counterbalancing the possible superficial and trivial effects which may be created by the other media because of their very nature.

Also, if the view is taken that every unit of recorded communication in a library, whether book or nonbook, is a channel of communication analogous with the channels of other systems, then libraries have by far the greater number of channels. This means that the individual has by far the greater chance of a discriminating choice by using the library. In terms of individual freedom, this is a tremendous advantage and one which should be taken full advantage of. Even if a reader limits his use to a small branch library, he is still likely to have a choice of some thousands of works immediately to hand, from which he may well borrow up to six or more at a time, against his channel choice of three in television. There is evidence of the lack of exercise of choice.[19]

The conclusion is that the historical development of libraries as systems open as freely as possible to everyone made them "mass" from that point of view, but in terms of disseminating information quickly to large audiences, they are completely outclassed by the new media. The library system should therefore concentrate on its strengths. It has the largest store of information and it should be prepared to put this at the disposal of the individual, tailored to meet his requirements.

If it is to compete directly with the other systems, it must deliver its goods directly into people's homes as does television, and it should be able to do so quickly to meet the demands of an individual inquiry, no matter what it is. In present-day terms, this may seem a tall order, but "near-technology" puts this within the realm of scientific possibility rather than science fiction. Speculators on future technological advances have envisaged worldwide telecommunications systems linked via satellites and fed to individual homes through consoles which are capable of receiving all types of messages—visual, aural, and print, as well as broadcasting messages.[20] The librarian's dream, therefore, must be that his data banks are totally linked by some such system and that an individual at his personal console can link them with his system and, on demand, receive the message he requires. There seems little doubt that much can be accomplished by electronic technology. The largest problem seems to be the electronic storage of information, and it is here that the computer as a communicatory tool is the hope. The theoretical prima facie case is that the reduction of information to the basic bit to suit the electronic speed of a computer has opened new words in the possibilities of storage of vast quantities of information in relatively small space and, provided we can devise suitable retrieval methods, it is the answer to many of the major problems in communications.

Such a development would underline the complementary nature of present systems since all the messages transmitted by them would be capable of reception on the communication console, with the obvious possiblity of creating "hard copy," if necessary.

NOTES

1. Parsons, E. A., *The Alexandrian Library* (American Elsevier Publishing Co., 1952), p. 136.
2. Jolliffe, H., *Public Library Extension Activities,* 2nd ed. (Library Association, 1968), p. 88.
3. Glasgow Public Libraries, *Annual Report of the City Librarian, 1970/71,* p. 40.
4. Great Britain, Statutes, *Public Libraries . . . Museums Act 1919* (His Majesty's Stationery Office, 1919).
5. Worsley, P., "Libraries and Mass Culture," *Library Association Record* (August 1967), pp. 259-267.
6. *British Books in Print, 1971* (Whitaker, 1971), p. iii; *Paperbacks in Print, 1972* (Whitaker, 1972), title page.
7. *Printing and the Mind of Man: Catalogue of a Display* (F. W. Bridges & Sons, 1963).
8. UNESCO, *Statistical Yearbook, 1972* (UNESCO, 1973), passim.
9. Luckham, B., *The Library in Society* (Library Association, 1971), p. 59.
10. UNESCO, *Statistical Yearbook, 1972,* pp. 870-875.
11. Luckham, B., and Orr, J., "Educational Broadcasting and Public Libraries," *Library Association Record* (January 1967), pp. 11-13.
12. Emmett, B. P., "The Television and Radio Audience in Britain," in McQuail, D., *Sociology of Mass Communications* (Penguin, 1972), pp. 208-209.
13. Sillitoe, A., ed., *Britain in Figures: A Handbook of Statistics,* 2nd ed. (Penguin, 1973), p. 174.

14. Emmett, "The Television and Radio Audience," p. 200.
15. Sillitoe, *Britain in Figures,* pp. 178-185.
16. *Annual Abstract of Statistics, 1960* (Her Majesty's Stationery Office, 1960), p. 83.
17. UNESCO, *Statistical Yearbook, 1972,* p. 883.
18. Emmett, "The Television and Radio Audience," pp. 211-212.
19. Ibid., p. 218.
20. Calder, N., ed., *The World in 1984,* 2 vols. (Penguin, 1965), passim.

Part Seven
RÉSUMÉ

Résumé

One of the dangers of taking a general and overall view of libraries, as has been done throughout this work, is the possibility of oversimplification. I realize that this has often happened. When dealing with the retrieval problem, for instance, the many difficulties encountered in author and descriptive cataloguing were, to some extent, brushed aside because it was held that it was the subject approach to knowledge which created the major problems for the indexer. While there has been oversimplification, it has been employed in order to concentrate on the most fundamental aspects of librarianship. This is what the systems approach achieves.

In Chapter 1, it was held that the application of systems theory developed a framework of general theory to enable one specialist to catch relevant communications from others.

The application of the general systems theory inevitably focuses attention on first principles of the system to which it is applied. There is, therefore, probably little which is new in any of the topics which have been covered, but there is perhaps a new conceptual way of viewing them which helps to identify objectives.

In concluding Chapter 1, a simple statement concerning the nature of librarianship was postulated. It is held that almost all of this postulate has been sustained in the more detailed examination of subsequent chapters and that little needs to be changed in redrafting it, but it might now be put in more certain terms.

A library is a communicatory tool created by man to complement his own deficient memory. It is a store for his graphically
produced records no matter what their format.

Its relationship with man is cyclic; it feeds his mind with information, much of which is reprocessed and returned to the
library. The library system therefore exhibits growth.

Its real effect on society is probabalistic, but over a length of
time it undoubtedly helps it to change.

In the long term, it is a complementary system to the other
communicatory tools of man, but in the short term it is competitive with other communication media.

Index

About the Author

J. M. Orr directs the School of Librarianship at Robert Gordon's Institute of Technology, Aberdeen, Scotland. He previously served as senior lecturer at the Loughborough Library School. Among his earlier publications is *Designing Library Buildings for Activity.*